NATURAL HEALING

NATURAL HEALING

Homeopathy • Herbalism • Relaxation • Stress Relief

SUE HAWKEY AND ROBIN HAYFIELD

HERMES
HOUSE

First published in 1999 by Hermes House

© Anness Publishing Limited 1999

Hermes House is an imprint of Anness Publishing Limited
Hermes House, 88-89 Blackfriars Road, London, SE1 8HA

This edition published in the USA by Hermes House, Anness Publishing Inc.,
27 West 20th Street, New York, NY 10011; (800) 354-9657

ISBN 1 84038 228 7

A CIP catalogue record for this book is available from the British Library

Publisher: *Joanna Lorenz*
Project Manager: *Helen Sudell*
Project Editor: *Fiona Eaton*
Editor: *Emma Gray*
Additional text: *Mark Evans, Jessica Houdret, John Hudson, Beverley Jollands, Nitya Lacroix*
Jacket Designer: *Simon Wilder*
Designers: *Bobbie Colgate Stone and Lilian Lindblom*
Illustrator: *Michael Shoebridge*
Photographer: *Don Last*
Production Controller: *Ben Worley*
Editorial Reader: *Hayley Kerr*

Additional photography by: *Alistair Hughes, Michelle Garrett, Lucy Mason and Debbie Patterson.*

Printed and bound in Singapore

1 3 5 7 9 10 8 6 4 2

Previously published as three separate volumes, *Homeopathy, Herbalism* and *Instant Calm*

CONTENTS

INTRODUCTION 8

LIKE FOR LIKE: THE ART OF HOMEOPATHY 14

HOW HOMEOPATHY WORKS 16

THE NATURE OF DISEASE: WHY WE BECOME ILL 18

THE VITAL FORCE AND THE IMMUNE SYSTEM 20

REMEDIES AND THEIR SOURCES 22

PROVINGS AND SYMPTOMS 24

CHOOSING THE CORRECT REMEDY 25

WHEN AND HOW TO USE REMEDIES 26

THE HOMEOPATHIC FIRST-AID KIT 28

REMEDIES FOR COMMON AILMENTS 30

First-aid Treatments 32

Treatments for Colds and Flu 36

Easing Ear Infections 40

Soothing the Eyes 41

Settling Gastric Upsets 42

Calming Boils and Abscesses 44

Relieving Toothache 45

Hay Fever and Other Allergies 46

Treating Babies and Children 48

Women's Health Problems 50

Emotional Issues 54

REMEDIES: THE MATERIA MEDICA 56

THE POWER OF PLANTS: THE ART OF HERBALISM   72

PLANTING A HERB GARDEN   74

PREPARING HERBS   76

    Gathering and Storing Herbs   78

    Making Teas   80

    Making Decoctions   81

    Making Tinctures   82

    Cold Infused Oils   83

    Herbs and Food   84

GUIDE TO HERBS AND THEIR USES   86

HERBAL RECIPES   110

    Preparing for a Big Day   112

    Coping with a Difficult Time   113

    Relieving PMT   114

    Easing Period Pain   115

    Helping with the Menopause   116

    Relaxing Tense Muscles   117

    Calming Anxiety   118

    Relieving Coughs and Colds   120

    Soothing a Sore Throat   121

    Recovering from Nervous Exhaustion   122

    Tonics for Convalescence   123

    Relieving Winter Blues   124

    Lifting Depression   125

    Digestives   126

    Hangover Remedies   128

    Relieving Headaches   129

    Revitalizing the Libido   130

    Enhancing Sleep   131

HEALTH AND HARMONY: NATURAL WELL-BEING 132

STRATEGIES FOR COPING WITH STRESS 134

RELAXING YOUR BODY 138

Loosening-up Exercises 140

Self-massage 146

Massage with a Partner 148

RELAXING YOUR MIND 150

Breathing to Calm the Mind 152

Ways of Gaining the Meditative State 153

Meditations: Guided Programmes 154

Meditation to Reduce Stress 156

NATURAL REMEDIES FOR STRESS 158

Using Essential Oils 160

Relaxing and Uplifting Essential Oils 162

RELIEVING THE SYMPTOMS OF STRESS 164

Tension Relievers 166

Instant Revitalizers 168

Muscle Fatigue Relievers 170

Backache Relievers 172

Relieving Anxiety 174

Dealing with Depression 175

Improving Self-worth 176

Getting a Good Night's Sleep 178

Libido Enhancer: Sensual Massage 180

Reducing Office Tension 184

For Confidence in Future Situations 186

USEFUL ADDRESSES 188

INDEX 190

INTRODUCTION

Health is, or should be, the most natural state of being. The origins of the word are linked with those of wholeness and healing, and it is that complete sense of harmony, of being whole, that brings true, vital health. This is also the ultimate aim of systems of natural healing, those that adopt a holistic view rather than the reductionist perspective that is evident in much of conventional modern medicine today.

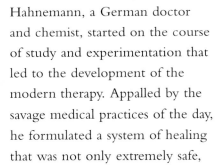

In recent years there has been a revival of interest in natural therapies, both in recognition of their tremendous value and as a move away from the impersonal approach and unwelcome side-effects of allopathic medicine. There are many ways in which natural therapies can be used at home as self-help remedies for a variety of common complaints and for simple first aid. However, it should not be forgotten that more complex and chronic conditions can and should be treated by professional practitioners of these therapies, and if you are in any doubt about a problem you should always seek qualified advice.

HOMEOPATHY

The traditions of natural medicine extend back over many centuries, and are based on a vast accumulation of practical knowledge. The principle underlying homeopathy has almost certainly been known for thousands of years, but it was not until the end of the 18th century that Samuel Hahnemann, a German doctor and chemist, started on the course of study and experimentation that led to the development of the modern therapy. Appalled by the savage medical practices of the day, he formulated a system of healing that was not only extremely safe, but scientifically based. His philosophy of disease and its cure through natural processes has changed very little from that day to this.

The principle of "like curing like", or "the law of similars", as it is sometimes called, decrees that though a substance may cause harm to a healthy person in large doses, in tiny doses it also has the potential to cure the same problem by stimulating the body's own natural energy, enabling it to heal itself.

The law is best illustrated by example. In the 19th century it was a custom among German women to take the herb Valerian regularly as a stimulant. The practice was much abused and caused overtaxing of the nervous system. Yet, given in minute homeopathic doses, Valerian relaxes the nervous system, calms the mind, and is one of homeopathy's main remedies for insomnia.

The doses used in homeopathy are so small that they cannot act directly on the physical body. Hahnemann considered that they act dynamically: that the energy of the remedy stimulates the natural healing energy of the body, if it is in a state of disharmony, in order to return to its former healthy state.

THE HEALING POWER OF HERBS

All over the world, in all cultures and throughout time, people have used plants not only as food but also for medicinal purposes. Traditional knowledge of herbal remedies used to be passed from generation to generation, but these days most of us have lost touch with the folklore of herbalism.

In modern industrialized societies we consume less natural plant material than our ancestors and have a lifestyle which is a far cry from theirs. At the same time, we have to deal not only with life's normal difficulties and changes, but also with many kinds of pollution, which add in various ways to the stresses on our minds and bodies. Fortunately, the countryside still produces wonderful herbs in abundance and many can be grown at home. Getting to know the plants growing around you can be a pleasurable form of relaxation.

Herbs, like people, are complex and variable organic structures made up of many parts. Each plant contains many different constituents combined to give a unique taste and range of actions. Particularly active constituents have been isolated and copied by pharmacists to produce medicines such as aspirin. However, using the whole plant has a more subtle effect and generates fewer side-effects. Herbalists therefore prefer to use the whole plant to treat the whole person. Each one of us is unique and reacts to life in a different way. Just as we each have preferences for different foods, we each respond best to particular herbs.

HERBS AND THE NERVOUS SYSTEM

It is our nervous system that co-ordinates all the complex activities that keep us well and help us adjust to constantly changing circumstances. Amongst the many properties of the plants described in this book, they can be used to support the nervous system. Herbalists call such plants nervines. They are useful when we feel debilitated and exhausted after illness, prolonged pressure or trauma. They improve the health and functioning of nervous tissue by invigorating and restoring it. Your choice will depend on whether nervous debility makes you hyperactive (choose relaxing nervines such as Skullcap, Vervain and Wood Betony) or restless, depressed and tired (choose stimulating nervines). Some plants such as coffee and tea stimulate the nervous system without nourishing it. Such over-stimulation is exhausting, so additional herbal stimulants are rarely used. There is a place for gently stimulating nervines, however. For example, Mugwort is beneficial during convalescence and Rosemary, by stimulating blood flow to the head, is useful in treating tension headaches.

You can use relaxing nervines to calm yourself down and prevent over-stimulation. Relaxing herbs such as Lemon Balm, Californian Poppy, Chamomile, Hops and Valerian will encourage rest and sleep. Korean and Siberian Ginseng, although they act as stimulants, are also very effective as short-term remedies for fatigue or debility, and are therefore known as adaptogens. Licorice and Borage support the adrenal glands in times of stress. Like all herbs, nervines have a range of actions – choose the one that fits your own symptoms. Knowing, growing, harvesting and drying herbs will improve your relationship with them, and you will find them more helpful.

You may discover that a symptom that is particularly troubling you can be treated by several different remedies. Studying all the actions of each herb can lead you to find one that will help other seemingly unconnected problems. This will be a particularly effective remedy for you.

A HEALTHY LIFESTYLE

All life follows a natural rhythm, with periods of activity followed by periods of rest. This is as it should be. Too much stimulation, or an over-reaction to stimulation, leads to a state of stress. Over time, you may reach a state of exhaustion, reducing your ability to react and cope appropriately with new stresses and jeopardizing your general health in many different ways.

Stress is recognized as one of the major factors affecting health in modern society and nearly everyone has felt its grasp at one time or another. Human beings have a wonderful natural system for maintaining balance, and the body is always striving to achieve a state of balance and inner harmony. But this balancing, adaptive energy is tested by stress, and is constantly being challenged. The increasing pace of modern life, the complexity of many professions, juggling the demands of work and family, changes and strains in relationships, all place considerable burdens on natural stress-management systems.

Stress is a normal part of life: in fact, a certain amount will do you no harm and is actually essential to motivation and personal development. Some people seem to be able to thrive on it, yet for others the pressure can become too much. The cumulative impact of events may sometimes mean that, eventually, you cannot go on coping and your body takes the strain.

There are plenty of things that you can do to help yourself cope better when life presents a challenge. The first step to improving the situation is to recognize it, and to accept your own limits. Actively reducing the amount of external stress you are under will, of course, be helpful, as well as looking at ways of easing its effects in the long term. Use the treatments and exercises described in this book to help you keep calm and relaxed while increasing your vitality and self-esteem.

LIKE FOR LIKE: *the Art of Homeopathy*

THE NAME "HOMEOPATHY" was coined by Samuel Hahnemann (1755-1843) from two Greek words that together mean "similar suffering", or "like cures like". In homeopathy, symptoms are seen not as the negative effects of illness but as the attempts of the body to resist disease. A remedy that produces such symptoms in a healthy person can be administered in minute amounts to encourage and support the patient's self-healing mechanisms, enabling them to combat the disease effectively.

HOW HOMEOPATHY WORKS

Homeopathy is not only an energy medicine but is also holistic. Homeopaths believe that the body is much more than the sum of its various parts and that the whole person should be treated. The mind, the emotions and all the various organs are interconnected. It would be unwise to treat one part without considering the whole person.

ENERGY WITHIN

The mechanics of this interconnection are extremely complex and almost impossible to understand in any detail. Luckily, in homeopathy we don't have to. We trust the process. Underlying the intricate physical and mental systems of the body is a refined and subtle system of energy, which is self-regulating and works efficiently almost all the time. We see it in action when we become ill. We feel unwell, have unpleasant symptoms, then we usually get better whether we take medicines or not. The body does its own healing, although it may sometimes need support when its own natural sources of healing energy are depleted or unbalanced.

THE HEALING PROCESS

The healing process can be compared to running a car. Modern cars are so efficient that, provided you maintain them properly, give them the right fuel and drive them sensibly, problems seldom arise. Then one

Above: Sometimes our bodies get stuck in disease, and we need a boost from a homeopathic remedy to get things moving again.

night, you forget to turn the lights off and the next morning the battery is flat and the car incapacitated. The only way to get the car moving again – the only cure – is to get a transfer of energy, in the form of a jump start from the battery of another car. Then all will be well. Homeopathy is a bit like getting a jump start! The energy sources are the remedies, used in accordance with the law of similars so that the body can run on all cylinders again.

A SAFE THERAPY

Many people turn to homeopathy because of their concerns about orthodox medicine, which is now very drug-orientated. Many drugs are very toxic and the side-effects in susceptible people can be very distressing. Even if the side-effects are not observable, the long-term problems associated with excessive use of drugs are little understood. Modern medicine seldom cures and it does not pretend to. It alleviates and palliates symptoms, and "manages" the illness, but since it addresses only the symptoms and seldom the disease itself, the results are often unsatisfactory. It is not holistic – consultants tend to be specialists in small parts of the system, ignoring the other parts.

Above: Remedies usually come in tablet form. But they can also be made up into creams and tinctures.

THE HOLISTIC PRINCIPLE

Homeopathy is safe to use and does not treat the removal of symptoms as an end in itself. Symptoms are considered as signs of distress or adjustment. The correct remedy removes the cause of the problem; the distressing symptoms will then fade away.

Homeopathy takes into account the nature of the person. It individualizes and recognizes that even if two people are diagnosed as having the same illness, they become ill in different ways and will need different remedies to effect a proper cure.

USING HOMEOPATHY

For chronic, or long-term, illnesses, you should consult a professional homeopath who will have had many years of training and subsequent experience. But for acute, non-serious ailments there is much good work that you can do yourself, with a small number of remedies and a book like this.

Above: Homeopathy individualizes. Different people are treated with different remedies for the same ailment.

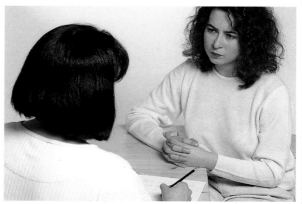

Above: You cannot treat chronic problems yourself. For these go and consult a qualified homeopath.

THE NATURE OF DISEASE: WHY WE BECOME ILL

We become ill when our energy is depleted or when we are out of harmony. The word "disease" should perhaps more accurately be written "dis-ease", indicating that we are not at ease. For a disease to be cured it is not necessary to give it a name. To cure homeopathically depends on an analysis of the symptoms. There is usually no need for a diagnosis, for it is said that there are no diseases, only "dis-eased" people.

SYMPTOMS

Except in life-threatening situations, symptoms – painful or distressing though they may be – are not the primary problem. They reflect a picture of how the system is making adjustments to heal itself.

For example, diarrhoea or vomiting is a necessary procedure for the body to rid itself of something it does not want in the quickest most effective way. Pain can be a warning that rest and stillness are immediately required, and it may also be a cry for help.

The intolerable itching of eczema does not specifically mean that you have a skin disease. Rather it means that there is imbalance in your whole system, and your body is pushing the problem to the safest possible place, as far away from the essential organs as possible. The skin is in fact an organ of elimination, and the suppressive use of steroids is not really helpful from a homeopathic point of view.

TREATING THE WHOLE PERSON

To cure well, it is necessary to see the whole picture and understand the person thoroughly. We are all individuals and have different weaknesses and susceptibilities. Some people are very robust and seldom become ill, apart from the odd cold. Others are over-sensitive and become run-down and sick after catching a slight chill or after some emotional upset. For some, their chest is their greatest weakness: every winter cold seems to turn to bronchitis. For others, it

Above: When we get ill, ease turns to dis-ease. Adjustments are needed to restore health.

is their digestion: the slightest unusual change in their diet causes an immediate upset.

Homeopathy acknowledges these differences and adjusts the treatment accordingly. The professional homeopath will prescribe "constitutionally" to try to strengthen the weak areas as well as the whole system.

CAUSES OF ILLNESS

There are many causes of disease. Some are obvious, such as the bruising or shock that follow an accident. A run-down and overworked constitution will probably not escape a winter flu epidemic.

Poor nutrition is another underlying cause. In the

Above: Mental and emotional stress can cause physical problems in the long run.

developed world, most people have enough to eat, but in these days of factory farming and junk food, the quality may not be good. Essential minerals and vitamins are often lacking.

Finally, illness may have an emotional cause. Stress is a major contributor to inner disharmony, which then manifests itself in physical ailments. Grief, fear, worry, depression and loneliness are not compatible with good health.

Homeopathy takes all these factors into account and, if possible, tries to mitigate them and strengthen the sufferer to be able to cope better with them.

Above: A good diet is essential to health. Apples and other fruit are especially good for you.

THE VITAL FORCE AND
THE IMMUNE SYSTEM

With so much battering from within and without, it may seem a wonder that we are not all permanently ill. Of course, many people are. Although many of the acute infectious diseases of the past have ceased to be a serious problem, their places have been taken by today's chronic diseases. Never has there been so much cancer and heart disease, eczema and asthma, or digestive problems such as irritable bowel disease. Our immune systems are overstretched in combating these problems.

Above: When the vital force is in perfect harmony, you will feel you can do anything!

THE IMMUNE SYSTEM

It is all too easy to ignore the incredible adaptability and intelligence of the immune system, which appears to make heroic efforts to keep us up and running despite considerable adversity. Hahnemann named this intelligence the "vital force". He described it as "the spirit-like force which rules in supreme sovereignty" It has also been described as "the invisible driver", overseeing the checks and balances of the immune system which operate to keep us in the best possible health.

THE VITAL FORCE AT WORK

Most of the time we are not aware of this balancing process – it is quite automatic and pre-programmed through our genetic inheritance. We can observe it in action when we contract an acute illness (one that arises suddenly) such as a fever or a cough. What we may not always realize is that the fever is necessary to burn up infection, and that the cough is there to prevent accumulation of mucus in the lungs. If the vital force cannot aid the curative process with acute diseases, it is forced to deal with

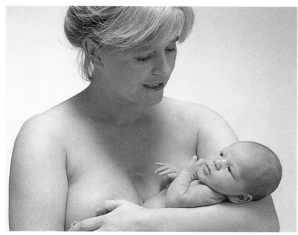

Above: We are all born with a vital force that oversees our health.

the problem through chronic disease (those that develop slowly, or are of long duration). Then it may need outside help.

THE SYMPTOM PICTURE

In its attempt to cure a disease, the vital force causes the body to produce symptoms. Homeopaths call this the symptom picture. These symptoms not only reflect what is going on inside but can also indicate what outside help or extra energy is required.

While it is true to say that in homeopathy we do not treat symptoms but the person who has them, we are nevertheless extremely interested in the symptoms. For it is through careful observation of the complete symptom picture that we will discover which remedy is required. In acute ailments, which are the subject of this book, the vital force will eventually cure, given

time. But by giving it a helping hand through noting what it needs via the symptoms and then giving the body an "energy fix" with the indicated remedy, the process can be speeded up considerably.

For example, suppose there is a flu epidemic and two children in a family catch it. The first child catches it very suddenly, literally overnight, and he develops a very high fever, with a red face and a dry burning heat all over his body. The second child's symptoms come on very slowly over several days. This child's fever is much lower, but she is shaky and shivery and her muscles ache all over. It's the same flu for both children, but the vital force has produced completely different symptoms. Each child therefore needs to be responded to in a different way. The homeopath will understand this and give the first child the remedy Belladonna and the second child Gelsemium.

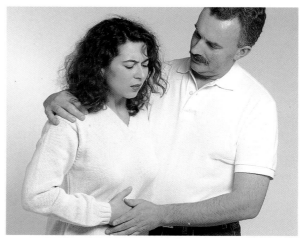

Above: All symptoms have meaning. Pain is a warning that there is disorder in the system.

REMEDIES AND THEIR SOURCES

The remedies used in homeopathy are derived from many sources. The majority are prepared from plants, but many minerals are also used and a few remedies are prepared from insect and snake poisons and other toxic substances. There is no need to be alarmed about their poisonous origins, for homeopathic remedies have been so diluted that no possible danger remains.

MAKING REMEDIES

The law of similars shows that the most powerful poisons can be turned into equally powerful remedies. Hahnemann discovered and used about a hundred remedies. About two thousand have now been described, but most professional homeopaths use only a fraction of that number.

To turn a substance into a remedy, so that the energy is tamed and harnessed, is an involved process usually carried out by a homeopathic pharmacy. The process itself is called potentization, and consists of two main procedures in alternation: dilution and succussion (or vigorous shaking).

Above: In homeopathy, all symptoms are taken into account in finding the correct remedy.

Right: The pills should be kept out of the light.

When you buy a remedy you will notice a number after its name, commonly 6, but also other numbers rising in a scale: 30, 200, 1M (1,000). Sometimes a "c", standing for centesimal (one hundredth) is written after the number. The number represents the potency, or the number of times the remedy has been diluted and succussed.

PREPARING HOMEOPATHIC REMEDIES

A remedy is prepared by dissolving a tincture of the original material – usually in alcohol. On the centesimal scale, the 6th potency means that the original substance has been diluted six times, each time using a dilution of one part in a hundred. This results in a remedy that contains only one part in a million million of the source material. Barely any molecules of the original substance will be present at this dilution, and if the potency is increased to 12c, there will be none left at all. Yet the greater the potency (or number of dilutions), the greater the power of the remedy seems to be. It may seem puzzling that homeopathy can possibly work at such a dilution, but you need to remember that it is an energy medicine and not primarily a physical one.

Between each dilution, the remedy is succussed. The phial (vial) in which it is being prepared is shaken

TISSUE SALTS

The 19th-century German doctor, Wilhelm Schussler, identified 12 vital minerals, or "tissue salts", essential to health. According to his theory, many diseases are associated with a deficiency of one or more of these substances, but can be cured by taking the tissue salts in minute doses, singly or in various combinations.

vigorously or banged a number of times. This is very important and ensures the release and transfer of energy from the original substance to the remedy. When the potentization is complete the remedy is preserved in alcohol, and a few drops can be added to a bottle of milk-sugar pills or a cream. This is called medicating the remedy, which is now ready to use.

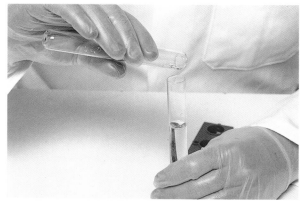

Above: The potentization of a remedy is carried out through a process of dilution and succussion (vigorous shaking and banging).

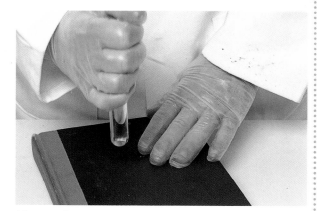

Above: The traditional way of succussing a remedy was to use an old leather-bound bible on which to bang the test tube.

PROVINGS AND SYMPTOMS

Almost all homeopathic remedies have been "proved", or tested, although practitioners gain additional knowledge of them from clinical experience. In a proving, a remedy is tested on a group of healthy people over a period of time, until they develop symptoms. Neither the supervisor nor the group should know what remedy they are proving. This is a true double blind test, conducted on scientific principles. The symptoms that the provers develop are tabulated and collated until a complete symptom picture is obtained. Now we know what the remedy can cure.

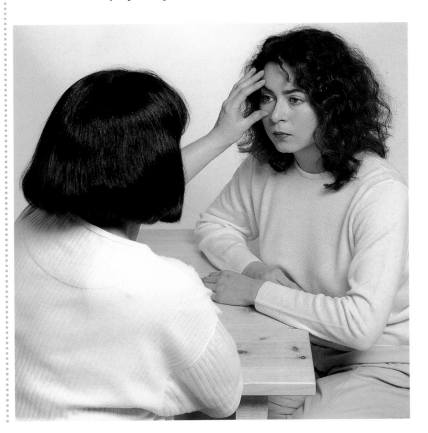

MATERIA MEDICA

Once proved, remedies can be used for all time. They do not go in and out of fashion. Almost all of Hahnemann's original hundred remedies are constantly in use today. Remedy pictures are detailed in large volumes called Materia Medica. Because so many symptoms for so many remedies have been proved over the last two hundred years, no homeopath could possibly remember them all. They are listed in another detailed book called The Homeopathic Repertory, which in effect is an index to the Materia Medica. These two books between them should cover almost all symptoms.

Left: In homeopathy, physical examinations are seldom necessary, but bright, sparkling eyes are a sign of good health.

CHOOSING THE CORRECT REMEDY

With a knowledge of Materia Medica, the homeopath is equipped to match the symptoms of the person with the symptom picture of the remedy. This is called finding the similimum (or similar).

PUTTING TOGETHER THE SYMPTOM PICTURE

Finding the correct remedy is like trying to arrange a perfect marriage. If the two partners are compatible, success is almost certain. If the remedy is a good match to the symptoms, the patient is going to feel a good deal better, the natural way. The words "I feel better in myself" are like music to the ears of the prescribing homeopath, because it means that the natural healing processes have been stimulated successfully, even if some of the physical symptoms remain. It should be only a short time before they too disappear.

The prescriber is like a detective looking for clues. Apart from the obvious general symptoms, such as fever, headache or a cough, you should note what are called the "modalities" – that is, what aggravates or alleviates the symptoms, or makes the person feel generally better or worse. They could include the need for warmth, or cool air, sitting up or lying down. Notice whether the person is thirsty or sweaty; whether the tongue is coated and the state of the breath. What kind of pain is it: throbbing, stitching or sudden stabs of intense agony?

Do the symptoms have an obvious cause? Did they arise after an emotional shock, or after catching a chill in a cold wind? Did they arise dramatically and suddenly in the middle of the night, or have they developed in rather a nondescript way over a number of days?

It is also very important to note the person's state of mind. For example, irritable people who just want to be left alone may need quite different remedies from those who want to be comforted and are easily consoled.

Above: Even members of the same family will have different susceptibilities to illness and react differently.

WHEN AND HOW TO USE REMEDIES

Many minor and self-limiting acute problems can be treated safely at home with a basic first-aid kit. However, for more serious long-term ailments, or if you feel out of your depth and really worried – especially if young children or old people are ill – seek help from your own homeopath or your doctor.

PROFESSIONAL HOMEOPATHS

Access to professional homeopaths is much easier nowadays and they can often do wonderful things for persistent and chronic disease. Qualified practitioners will have completed three or four years' training.

Above: You may feel unsure about treating very young children, but homeopathy usually works brilliantly on them, and can be safely used from birth.

HOMEOPATHIC FIRST-AID

What you are trying to do is help the body help itself. Sometimes there may not be a great deal you can do – a well-established cold is going to mean several days of suffering whether you intervene or not. In other cases, the sooner you act, the better: for instance, if you give Arnica (either in pill form, or rubbed-in cream if appropriate) immediately after a bad fall for the bruising and shock, the results will be very impressive.

You can often limit the duration or intensity of suffering, such as in fever, sepsis (pus-forming bacteria), pain, indigestion and many other conditions. Moreover, there will be many satisfying times when the problem is aborted or cured altogether.

Once you see an improvement, the vital force needs no further help and you can stop the remedy. You will do no harm if you don't, but there is no point in giving more energy than needed. In homeopathy "less is more".

GIVING THE REMEDY

The 6th and 30th potencies are most useful for home use. As a rough rule of thumb, use a 6c three or four times a day, or a 30c once or twice daily until symptoms improve. One pill at a time is all that is necessary and there is no need to reduce the dosage for children.

Above: After placing a remedy on your tongue, suck it for about 30 seconds before crunching.

In serious situations such as a high fever or after an accident, you can give a remedy every half-hour if necessary. You can't overdose in acute situations and if you don't get a good reaction within a day or overnight, you may want to consider a second remedy. Never worry about giving the wrong remedy: it will either work or it won't. If it doesn't, you will have done no harm.

Sometimes the symptoms may change after giving a remedy, so that a new picture emerges. You then need to find a new remedy to fit the new picture. If the situation improves, or the picture is unclear, watch and wait. Only intervene if you feel you need to.

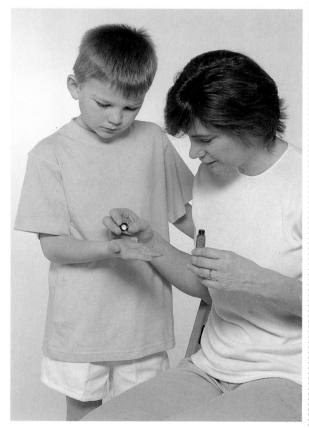

Above: The simplest way to give a child a remedy is to pour one tablet from the cap into the patient's hand and then place it directly into the mouth.

THE HOMEOPATHIC FIRST-AID KIT

It's a good idea to keep a basic first aid-kit in the house so that you are prepared for all emergencies. Many remedies are available from health food shops or some chemists. But there may not be a source near you and it is amazing how many homeopathic situations arise outside shop-opening hours.

OBTAINING REMEDY KITS

You can obtain a remedy kit from a good homeopathic pharmacy. All pharmacies will supply their own kits, or make one up to your own specifications. This can be as big or small as you like.

This book describes 42 remedies. Many of these you may never need, so it would be wise to begin with about half that number: these will cover most common situations. You can then add more remedies as you become more confident and experienced.

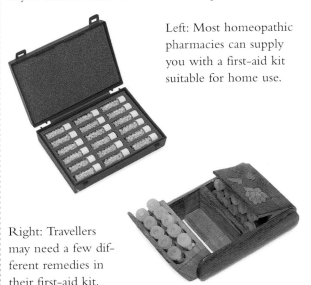

Left: Most homeopathic pharmacies can supply you with a first-aid kit suitable for home use.

Right: Travellers may need a few different remedies in their first-aid kit.

Above: Calendula cream is the best remedy to use on open cuts and sores.

YOUR FIRST-AID KIT SHOULD INCLUDE:

ARNICA CREAM – for bruises

CALENDULA CREAM – for cuts and sores

RESCUE REMEDY TINCTURE – for major emergencies

ECHINACEA TINCTURE - for the immune system

PLUS THESE BOTTLES OF PILLS:

ACONITE – for fevers, coughs and colds

APIS – for bites and stings

ARNICA – for bruising or shock following accidents

ARSENICUM – for digestive upsets, food poisoning

BELLADONNA – for high fever, headache

BRYONIA – for dry coughs and fevers

CHAMOMILLA – for teething, colic

FERRUM PHOS – for colds and flu, anaemia

GELSEMIUM – for flu and anxiety

HEPAR SULPH – for sore throats, infected wounds

HYPERICUM – for injuries

IGNATIA – for grief and emotional upsets

LEDUM – for puncture wounds, bites and stings

LYCOPODIUM – for anxiety, digestive problems

MERCURIUS – for sepsis

NUX VOMICA – for hangovers, nausea, indigestion

PHOSPHORUS – for digestive problems, nosebleeds

PULSATILLA – for ear infections, fevers, eye problems

RHUS TOX – for sprains and strains, rashes

RUTA – for injuries to tendons and bones

RESCUE REMEDY

Although not strictly a homeopathic treatment, Rescue Remedy is one of Dr Edward Bach's Flower Remedies. These flower essences are a series of gentle plant remedies which are intended to treat various emotional states, regardless of the physical disorder. For practical purposes, the Rescue Remedy is the finest treatment available for alleviating symptoms of shock. It is a compound of five of Dr Bach's original remedies, namely Impatiens, Star of Bethlehem (*Ornithogatum umbellatum*), Rock rose (*Cistus*), Cherry plum (*Prunus cerasifera*) and *Clematis vitalba*.

Impatiens.

Cherry plum.

Clematis.

Rock rose.

Star of Bethlehem.

REMEDIES FOR COMMON AILMENTS

Many straight forward problems can be treated at home using homeopathy. For each one, a number of remedies are listed on the following pages that are likely to be most helpful. Read the remedy picture carefully and choose the one that seems to make the best "fit" with the symptoms you have observed. When you have selected your remedy, double-check it with the more detailed description in the Materia Medica section towards the end of the section.

HOW TO TAKE THE REMEDY

Once you have chosen the remedy, empty one pill into the cap of the bottle. If more than one lands in the cap, tip the others back into the bottle without touching them.

Drop the pill on to a clean tongue – that is, you should take the remedy at least 10 minutes before or after eating, drinking or cleaning your teeth. The pill should be sucked for about 30 seconds before being crunched and swallowed. Remedies for babies can be crushed to a powder in an envelope and given on a teaspoon.

ECHINACEA

Echinacea angustifolia, or the purple cornflower, is a native American herb. It is a general tonic for the immune system, and is particularly useful to take if you have been feeling run down for a while.

Above: Sympathy and a hug is sometimes the best medicine.

Right: Homeopathy is an exacting science.

FIRST-AID TREATMENTS

Homeopathic remedies can be used as first-aid treatment in many situations, but serious injuries should always receive expert medical attention. If you are worried, call for help first, then give the appropriate remedy while you wait for help to arrive.

BRUISES

The very first remedy to think of after any injury or accident is *ARNICA*. For local bruising, where the skin is unbroken, apply Arnica cream, and whether you use the cream or not you can give an Arnica pill as often as you think necessary, until the bruising starts to go down. Arnica is also

wonderful in cases of shock. If the person is dozy (woozy) or unconscious, crush the remedy first and place the powder directly on the lips.

Where there is serious shock, or in any real emergency, use *RESCUE REMEDY*. This can be used either alone or with Arnica in cases of physical trauma. Place a few drops of the Rescue Remedy straight on to the lips or tongue, every few minutes if necessary.

If the injury results in pains shooting up the arms or legs, try *HYPERICUM*. This remedy is very useful where very sensitive areas have been hurt, such as the toes, fingers, lips and ears.

If the joints or bones have been hurt, *RUTA* may be more effective than Arnica, which is more of a soft tissue remedy.

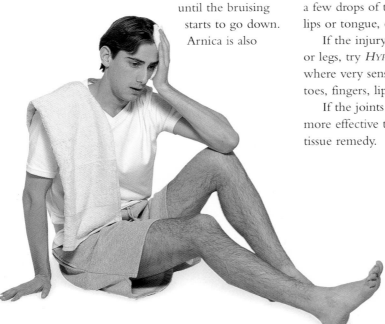

Above: After any injury or shock, the first remedy to think of is Arnica.

Above: The herb Rue, used in the remedy Ruta.

CUTS, SORES AND OPEN WOUNDS

The first priority is to clean the area gently but thoroughly to remove any dirt. If the wound is very deep, it may need stitches and you should seek medical help. Once the wound is clean, gently apply some *CALENDULA* cream. *HYPERCAL* cream, which is a mixture of Calendula and *HYPERICUM*, will do equally well. If necessary, add a dressing to keep the wound clean.

PUNCTURE WOUNDS

Such injuries can arise from animal or insect bites, pins, needles and nails, or from standing on a sharp instrument such as a garden fork (rake).

If the wound becomes puffy and purple and feels cold, yet the pain is eased by cold compresses, *LEDUM* is the best remedy. If there are shooting pains, which travel up the limbs along the tracks of the nerves, then *HYPERICUM* should be used.

SPRAINS AND STRAINS

For general muscle strains, resulting from lifting heavy weights or excessive physical exercise such as aerobics or long hikes over hilly countryside, *ARNICA* will almost always be extremely effective. For deeper injuries where the joints are affected, as a result of a heavy fall or a strong football tackle, use *RUTA*.

For even more severe sprains, especially to the ankles or wrists, where the pain is agony on first moving the joint but eases with gentle limbering up, *RHUS TOX* should be very helpful.

For injuries where the slightest movement is extremely painful and hard pressure eases the pain, use *BRYONIA*.

Above: Rhus tox can be a very good remedy for sprains, especially to the ankles or wrists.

FRACTURES

Once a broken bone has been set, use *SYMPHYTUM* daily, night and morning, for at least three weeks. This will not only ease the pain but also speed up the knitting of the bones.

Above: Comfrey, used in the remedy Symphytum.

BURNS

Severe burns need urgent medical assistance: do not delay, especially in the case of children and babies.

For minor burns and scalds, *CALENDULA* or *HYPERCAL* cream is very soothing, especially if applied straight away. If the pain remains, or the burn is more severe, take one pill of the remedy *CANTHARIS* every few hours until the pain eases. If shock is involved or you have a hysterical child, also use *ARNICA* (in pill form) and/or *RESCUE REMEDY*.

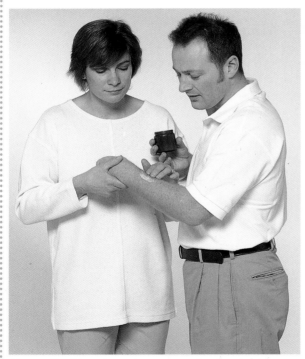

Above: For bites that come up as a bruise, Arnica cream can be very effective.

Above: The herb St John's Wort, used in the remedy Hypericum.

BITES AND STINGS

For minor injuries, apply *CALENDULA* or *HYPERCAL* cream. If the wound looks bruised, use *ARNICA*, either as a cream or in pill form. If the wound becomes very swollen and looks red and puffy, use *APIS*.

For injuries to sensitive areas, such as fingers, especially if shooting pains can be felt, *HYPERICUM* will be a useful remedy. *LEDUM* would be preferable if the wound is puffy and cold to the touch, yet is helped by cold compresses.

TRAVEL SICKNESS

Many people get seasick in rough weather and some, especially children, are also air-sick or car-sick. The symptoms are usually eased by the remedy *COCCULUS*.

FEAR OF FLYING

For sheer terror, use *ACONITE* and/or *RESCUE REMEDY* before you go to the airport and then as often as you need to during the flight. If you shake with anxiety, try *GELSEMIUM*.

If the problem is more a question of claustrophobia, the fear of being trapped in a narrow space, *ARG NIT* should be very useful.

VISITS TO THE DOCTOR OR DENTIST

For any surgery or dental work where bruising and shock to the system are involved, you cannot go wrong with *ARNICA*. Take one pill just before

Above: Rescue Remedy can be wonderful in states of extreme anxiety, and in emotional shock.

treatment and one pill three times a day for as long as you need it.

For wounds that are slow to heal, or where there is sepsis, apply *CALENDULA* or *HYPERCAL* cream. If there are injuries to the nerves, the symptoms of which may be shooting pains along the nerve tracks, *HYPERICUM* can be helpful.

Where post-operative bleeding is a problem, such as after a tooth extraction, *PHOSPHORUS* should stop it. Phosphorus is also very useful for that post-anaesthetic "spacey" feeling that won't go away. Sometimes, persistent nausea may remain. *IPECAC* can be wonderful in such circumstances.

For pre-dentist nerves, *ARG NIT* and *GELSEMIUM* are two of the best remedies.

Above: The herb Arnica, used in the remedy of the same name.

TREATMENTS FOR COLDS AND FLU

Most colds, unless nipped in the bud, take their course and should clear up in a week or so. Flu can be much more debilitating, but a good remedy can often ameliorate the symptoms.

COLDS AND FLU

If flu comes on suddenly, often at night and perhaps after catching a chill, with symptoms of high fever and profuse sweating, *ACONITE* is a good remedy. If the symptoms are similarly sudden and with a high temperature, but with redness, burning heat and a headache, the remedy is more likely to be *BELLADONNA*.

Above: At the first sign of a head cold, try Arsenicum or Allium cepa.

For flu that appears more slowly, accompanied by extreme thirst, irritability and the desire to be left alone, *BRYONIA* will be very useful.

Probably the most widely used remedy in flu is *GELSEMIUM*. The most pronounced symptoms are shaking with shivering, aching muscles and general weakness. Where aching bones are prominent, use *EUPATORIUM*.

Above: Kali bich can be a good remedy for blocked sinuses where there is pain and a green stringy discharge.

For head colds with sneezing and an acrid nasal discharge, *ALLIUM CEPA* or *ARSENICUM* should help. If the sinuses are also affected and there is a lot of yellow-green mucus which appears in globules or looks sticky and stringy, use *KALI BICH.*

Above: The red onion is used to make the remedy Allium cepa.

For a general tonic, both during and after the flu, when symptoms are not very well defined and there is general malaise, try *FERRUM PHOS.*

COUGHS AND CROUP
For very harsh, dry, violent coughs, which may appear suddenly and may be worse at night, use *ACONITE.* For a hard, dry painful cough, which seems to be helped by holding the chest very tightly and also by long drinks of cold water, use *BRYONIA.*

For deep-seated, dry, spasmodic coughs that may end in retching or even vomiting, use *DROSERA.* Painful, barking coughs, which produce thick yellow-green mucus, may be helped by *HEPAR SULPH.* For coughs that are suffocating and sound like a saw going through wood, try *SPONGIA.* Where there is a lot of mucus seemingly trapped in the chest, try *ANT TART.*

Croup is a horrible sounding dry cough that affects small children. The main remedies are *ACONITE, HEPAR SULPH* and *SPONGIA.* Try each in turn, if it is difficult to differentiate between the symptoms.

Above: Natural sponge.

Above: Harsh, dry coughs are often helped by Bryonia.

37

If the sore throat feels worse on the left side and swallowing liquids is particularly painful, use *LACHESIS*. Use *LYCOPODIUM* if the throat is worse on the right side or the pain moves from right to left; warm drinks may be comforting.

For a sore throat accompanied by offensive breath and saliva, plus sweatiness and thirst, try *MERCURIUS*. For throats that look dark and red and feel as if a hot lump has got stuck inside, try *PHYTOLACCA*.

FEVERS

Fevers, particularly in children, whose temperatures may be quite high, may seem alarming, but it should

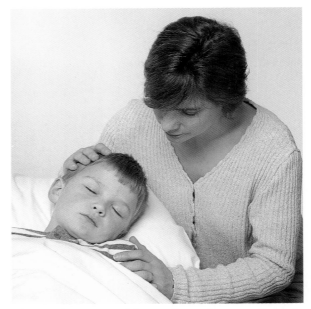

Above: The most useful remedies at the start of a high fever in children are Aconite and Belladonna.

Above: There are many remedies for sore throats. Check the symptoms carefully before deciding.

SORE THROATS

If a sore throat starts suddenly, often during the night, perhaps following a chill and accompanied by a high temperature, try *ACONITE*. If the throat burns and throbs painfully and looks very red, it may be eased by *BELLADONNA*.

For a sore throat that looks very swollen and puffy, with a stinging pain, try *APIS*. *HEPAR SULPH* can be used for an extremely painful throat that feels as if there is a fish bone stuck in it, making it very hard to swallow.

The lime of oyster shells (above) and flowers of sulphur (right) are heated together to make the remedy for Hepar sulph.

be remembered that they are the body's natural response to dealing with and burning up infection.

The two main remedies for high fevers that appear suddenly and often dramatically are *ACONITE* and *BELLADONNA*. There is usually thirst and sweat present in the Aconite picture, while Belladonna cases will be characterized by a dry skin, redness and a throbbing pain in the affected area.

If the fever appears more slowly and the person is irritable, wants to be left alone and is very thirsty for long drinks of cold water, try *BRYONIA*. For flu-like fevers, with shivering, weakness and aching muscles, use *GELSEMIUM*. *FERRUM PHOS* can be used in milder fevers, with no particularly distinctive symptoms.

PULSATILLA is really useful in children's fevers, where the child is very emotional, clingy and weepy and wants to be held and comforted.

Above: The North American plant, Gelsemium.

EASING EAR INFECTIONS

Acute earaches are most common in young children. They need to be treated quickly, as an infection within the middle ear can be both painful and damaging. Speedy home help can be very useful, but get medical help if the earache worsens or persists.

One of the most soothing remedies is *VERBASCUM* oil. Pour a few drops into a warmed spoon, and insert gently into the child's ear.

For sudden and violent pains, accompanied by fever which usually start at night, use *ACONITE*. Where there is a fever with a sudden and violent appearance and the ear throbs and looks very red, *BELLADONNA* will cure it.

For earaches where there is great pain and the child is exceptionally irritable, use *CHAMOMILLA*. *FERRUM PHOS* is indicated where the pain comes on slowly and there are no other particularly distinguishing symptoms. For very painful and sore earaches with some discharge of yellow-green mucus, when the child is also chilly and irritable, use *HEPAR SULPH*. For pains that extend to the throat and sinuses, accompanied by sweating, thirst and bad breath, use *MERCURIUS*.

PULSATILLA suits children who prefer to be kept cool and seem to feel better when they are held and comforted. The earaches may come and go without particular reason.

Above: Verbascum.

Left: An effective cure for children's earaches is Verbascum oil.

SOOTHING THE EYES

Overwork, pollutants, viral and bacterial infections can all affect the delicate tissues in and around the eyes. Stress and fatigue tend to aggravate these problems by weakening the immune system's ability to fight off infection.

ACONITE is indicated when the eye feels hot and dry, perhaps after catching a cold in it. It may feel as if a piece of grit is irritating it. *APIS* is a good remedy to use when the eyelids look puffy and swollen and the discomfort is relieved by cold compresses.

For eyes that look red and bloodshot and are over-sensitive to light, *BELLADONNA* is indicated, while *EUPHRASIA* is one of the very best remedies for sore and burning eyes. It can also be used in an eyebath, as it can be obtained in a diluted tincture.

One of the best remedies for styes is *PULSATILLA*, which should be used for eye infections with a sticky yellow discharge.

When treating eye injuries, *SYMPHYTUM* can be used where there has been a direct blow to the eyeball. For general injuries to the eye, *ARNICA* is often the most helpful remedy to ease the bruising. *LEDUM* will come into its own if, after an injury, the eye is cold and puffy, yet the pain is eased by cold compresses.

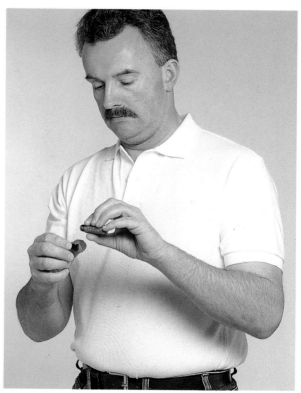

Above: Aconite can be good in some eye infections – but check the symptoms first.

Left: Comfrey, used in the remedy Symphytum.

SETTLING GASTRIC UPSETS

The main symptoms of stomach and intestinal infections are pain, wind (gas), nausea, vomiting or diarrhoea. Bear in mind that vomiting and diarrhoea are natural processes by which the body rids itself quickly of unwanted material, so these symptoms need to be treated only if they are persistent. Such problems can arise at any time and may be due to food poisoning or may just be a reaction to unfamiliar food, perhaps while you are on vacation.

UPSET STOMACH

The great stand-by remedy is *ARSENICUM*. Other symptoms which may accompany diarrhoea or vomiting are excessive weakness, coldness and restlessness. *MAG PHOS* is an excellent remedy for general abdominal cramps which are helped by doubling up and by warmth.

For constant nausea which is unrelieved by vomiting, use *IPECAC*. *NUX VOMICA* is a good remedy for gastric upsets where nothing really seems to happen. Undigested food lies like a dead weight in the stomach – if only it could be vomited, you would feel better.

PHOSPHORUS can be a useful remedy for diarrhoea that runs like a tap, especially if there is a sensation of burning in the stomach. You may crave cold water, but it is vomited up as soon as it has warmed up in the stomach.

Above left: A piece of Arsenopyrite, containing the metallic mineral arsenic, used in the remedy Arsenicum.

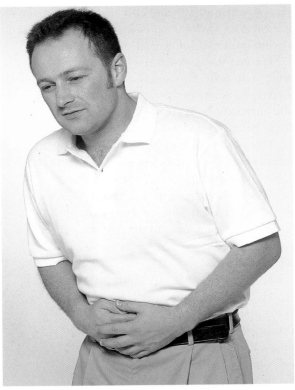

Above: In food poisoning, where there is pain and vomiting or diarrhoea, think of Arsenicum.

INDIGESTION

The symptoms of indigestion are heartburn, wind (gas) and cramping pains. They are usually caused by eating too much or too quickly, especially if you are eating very rich food and drinking alcohol.

The most useful remedy is *NUX VOMICA*. The digestive system seems stuck, heavy and sluggish and the feeling is that you would feel much better if the undigested food would move – up or down or out!

Another remedy that is sometimes helpful is *LYCOPODIUM*. Trapped wind (gas) can cause extreme discomfort. Late afternoon or early evening is often the worst time for this, and the feeling is sometimes accompanied by anxiety. The remedy often works well on people whose gastric system is the weakest part of their constitution.

Above: Lycopodium.

Left: Nux vomica can be a great remedy in indigestion – especially after a good night out!

CALMING BOILS AND ABSCESSES

Sometimes, an area of the skin becomes inflamed and gathers pus. This usually happens around a hair follicle. The build-up of pus can cause acute pain before it comes to a head as a boil or abscess, or until the pus is absorbed by the body.

In the early stages of a boil or abscess, when it looks red and angry and throbs painfully, *BELLADONNA* is often the best remedy. Later when it starts becoming septic (infected) and even more painful as the pus increases, use *HEPAR SULPH*.

If the boil seems very slow in coming to a head, *SILICA* should be used to speed up the process. This remedy is also helpful as a daily tissue salt for unhealthy skin that keeps producing boils. The nails may also be unhealthy, breaking and peeling too easily.

Above: Silica is a remedy that can often help boils come to a head.

Above: The original proving for Silica was rock crystal.

RELIEVING TOOTHACHE

There is probably no worse agony than toothache, as the area is so sensitive. In most cases, a visit to the dentist will be essential, but the following remedies may help with the pain in the meantime.

For sudden and violent pains, perhaps precipitated by a cold, ACONITE may be helpful. If the area looks very red and throbs violently, BELLADONNA should be used. For abscesses, where pus is obviously present and the saliva tastes and smells foul, the best remedy is likely to be MERCURIUS. If you are prone to abscesses and your teeth are generally not very strong, SILICA should be used to strengthen the system.

For pain that lingers after a visit to the dentist, take ARNICA or HYPERICUM. If the pain is accompanied by extreme irritability, CHAMOMILLA should be used.

HEPAR SULPH is a suitable remedy for extreme septic states (infected areas), where bad temper is a prominent symptom. Another remedy for toothache where there are spasmodic shooting pains is MAG PHOS.

Above: There are several remedies that can help with toothache, but you still need to visit the dentist.

Above: St John's Wort, for the remedy Hypericum.

Above right: Arnica

HAY FEVER AND OTHER ALLERGIES

Over the last 20 or 30 years there has been an enormous increase in allergies, which might be better described as an over-sensitivity of the body to substances that cannot be easily assimilated. Hay fever, eczema, asthma, irritable bowel disease, chronic fatigue and other chronic diseases have reached almost epidemic proportions.

Above: Allergies, or over-sensitivity to certain foods, are becoming increasingly common. Dairy products and wheat-based foods seem to cause the most problems.

HOMEOPATHY AND CHRONIC DISEASE

No one knows precisely what causes these problems. There are undoubtedly a number of reasons. Toxicity overload is almost certainly one. The body simply cannot cope with the huge number of chemicals and drugs which it was not designed to absorb. Another reason is probably deficient nutrition. Many foods are now so over-processed that they do not contain sufficient minerals and vitamins to allow the body to function efficiently.

Homeopathy can often work wonders in correcting the many imbalances and weaknesses which result. Obviously, you should also take care to avoid toxic substances wherever possible, and eat a good, varied diet. The homeopathy needed to cure chronic ailments is complex and time-consuming, and beyond the scope of this book.

You will need help from a professional homeopath.

However, there is a certain amount you can do to alleviate the discomfort of acute hay fever symptoms.

HAY FEVER

Hay fever is rather a misnomer, for there are many other substances apart from hay which can trigger the well-known symptoms of watering eyes and runny nose, itchiness and sneezing. The problem may last for a few weeks, a few months or all year round, depending on the cause.

EUPHRASIA and *ALLIUM CEPA* are two of the most effective acute remedies. If the problem is centred in the eyes, with even the tears burning, Euphrasia is the remedy to use. However, if the nasal symptoms are worse, with constant streaming and an acrid discharge, then try Allium cepa.

Another remedy that is sometimes useful when there are constant burning secretions from the mucous membranes is *ARSENICUM*. This remedy also has a "wheezy" picture, so think of it when there is hay fever with asthmatic breathing, often worse at night.

Above: There is no substitute for a healthy diet.

Above: The best remedy for hay fever, when the eyes are worst affected, is usually Euphrasia.

Above: Allium cepa.

TREATING BABIES AND CHILDREN

Children tend to respond very well to homeopathy and are a joy to treat. There is no substitute for constitutional treatment from an experienced professional homeopath, so that the overall immune system can be boosted as much as possible, but with a good stock of remedies there is much you can do at home in acute situations.

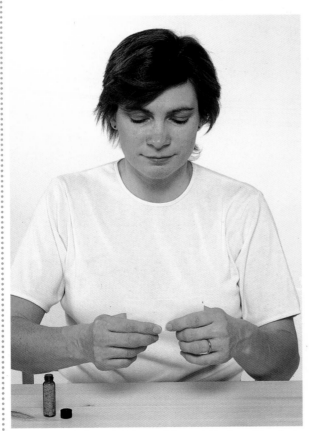

Above: For babies, it is essential to crush the tablet first.

CHILDREN AND HOMEOPATHY

The best start you can give a child is love and security, breast milk for as long as practical, a good varied diet, as few drugs as possible, and homeopathy. Young children often have dramatic acute conditions, such as fevers. Usually there is nothing to worry about if you are well informed, have professional support and have access to remedies. The dosage is the same as for adults, but remember to crush the pills first for babies.

TEETHING

The most widely used remedies for teething pains are *CHAMOMILLA* and *PULSATILLA*. Chamomilla is an "angry" remedy and suits bad-tempered babies best. These are the ones that drain you of sympathy because you have had so many sleepless nights and you feel so helpless. Only picking them up and carrying them around soothes them. Pulsatilla children respond differently – they are softer, weepy and invite your sympathy. They feel better and are soothed by being cuddled. They also need to be kept cool.

FEVERS

Many small children get fevers with very high temperatures, as they burn up infection in the most efficient way. Seek help if the fever goes on for more

Above: For teething discomfort, Chamomilla or Pulsatilla are two of the most effective remedies.

than 24 hours, especially if there is a violent headache or drowsiness. ACONITE and BELLADONNA are the best general high fever remedies.

CROUP

This harsh, dry cough is very disturbing in small children, but usually sounds far worse than it is. There are three main remedies for croup. ACONITE can be used for particularly violent and sudden coughs, which are often worse at night. For harsh coughs that sound like sawing through wood, SPONGIA is the remedy. For a rattly chest with thick yellow-green mucus, possibly marked by irritability and chilliness, use HEPAR SULPH.

COLIC

This trapped wind (gas) and digestive pain can be very upsetting for a small baby. The baby may try to curl up to ease the pain, and warmth and gentle massage should help. MAG PHOS is a useful remedy to try.

Above: The herb Chamomile, used in the remedy Chamomilla.

Above: Deadly nightshade, used in the remedy Belladonna.

Above: For colicky babies, Mag Phos often soothes the pain as well as the nervous system.

WOMEN'S HEALTH PROBLEMS

A woman's weakest area often seems to be connected with her reproductive system and its associated hormones. The system is as delicate and intricate as a watch movement, but unfortunately it is often treated rather heavy-handedly by modern medicine. Many problems can be resolved by constitutional homeopathic treatment, as well as by dietary adjustments. For non-persistent conditions, homeopathic self-help will ease much distress.

ANAEMIA

Anaemia is usually caused by an iron deficiency and manifests itself through weakness, pallor and lack of stamina. The most vulnerable times are during pregnancy or after excessive blood loss due to heavy periods. Iron pills supplied by your doctor often severely upset the bowels, so gentler methods are preferable. Eat foods rich in iron and try organic iron preparations which can be obtained from health food shops. *FERRUM PHOS* should also be used daily.

CYSTITIS

Many women are familiar with the burning agony of urinating when they have a bladder infection. Cranberry juice or sodium bicarbonate can often help. Two of the most useful remedies are *CANTHARIS* and *APIS*. Use Cantharis as a general remedy. Apis can be helpful when the last drops in urination hurt the most.

MASTITIS

Mastitis means inflammation of the breast and occurs commonly during breast-feeding. It can be painful but is not normally serious. Breast-feeding does not have to stop because of it. Homeopathy is usually very successful in curing the inflammation.

Above: A woman's hormonal balance is very finely tuned and is easily upset.

PHYTOLACCA has a special affinity with the breast area and is the most important remedy for the condition. The breast may feel lumpy as well as being swollen. The nipple may be cracked and particularly sensitive. If the breast looks very red and throbs painfully, BELLADONNA should be considered. PULSATILLA is also a remedy to think of when emotional issues are uppermost – especially when you feel unsupported and weepy.

Above: Iron-rich foods include red meat, egg yolks, legumes, shellfish and parsley.

Above: One of the best all-round remedies for mastitis is Phytolacca.

Above: The honey-bee, used in the remedy Apis.

PRE-MENSTRUAL TENSION (PMT)

Most women are familiar with the mood changes that arise just before an oncoming period. But for an unfortunate few, more extreme symptoms of depression, anger and weepiness can appear, sometimes as much as a week or more before the flow begins. A visit to a professional homeopath can often be of great benefit, but there are some remedies that you might try yourself at home to alleviate some of these very distressing symptoms.

PULSATILLA is an excellent remedy if weeping and the feeling of neediness is prominent. *SEPIA* should be used where there is anger and exhaustion, and even indifference towards your family. *LACHESIS* is helpful for the more extreme symptoms of violent anger, jealousy and suspicion.

Above: Meditation can be an excellent way to relax the nervous system.

PERIOD PAINS

If your period pains are consistently bad, you will need to consult a homeopath. For occasional pains, there are a number of self-help remedies from which you can choose. The three PMT remedies mentioned above, *PULSATILLA, SEPIA* and *LACHESIS,* should be considered if the emotional symptoms described fit, and seem over-riding.

For pains that respond to warmth and make you want to curl up, *MAG PHOS* should be helpful. For very severe pains, with bad cramping, *VIBURNUM OPULUS* can be a great painkiller.

Above: PMT mood swings are not uncommon. Check your symptoms to find a remedy that might help.

MENOPAUSE AND HOT FLUSHES

Unfortunately, there is now a great tendency for doctors to treat the menopause as a disease, when it simply marks the end of a woman's childbearing years. Because of this there has been a great rush into Hormone Replacement Therapy (HRT). In fact, the symptoms of an out-of-balance menopause can usually be treated very successfully in a more natural way through nutrition and homeopathy. The remedies most often used are again *PULSATILLA, SEPIA* and *LACHESIS*. They can often be prescribed according to the personality and state of mind of the woman, as described previously for PMT.

Above: Dried Cramp Bark, a herb used in the remedy Viburnum opulus.

Above: The menopause is not an illness and does not have to be an ordeal. Pulsatilla is often used by homeopaths, with very good results.

EMOTIONAL ISSUES

We underrate at great risk the part our emotions play in our well-being. Much disease
can arise from the disharmony in our lives. This is even more likely if we are unable to express
our emotions and our feelings remain buried within us. Just as joy, laughter and the feeling of being
cared for can keep us in good health, the opposite feelings of sadness, hatred,
grief and insecurity are at the root of many illnesses.

Above: The most useful remedy for emotional upsets, where you always
feel better for being comforted, is Pulsatilla.

EMOTIONAL TURMOIL

It is almost a daily occurrence for
a homeopathic practitioner to hear
words like "I've never really got
over my father's death," or "I've
never properly felt well since my
divorce." It is important for good
health not to allow such wounds
to fester too deeply. Homeopathy
can often assist both in chronic
conditions and in acute ones
where you feel you need help.

In any emotional situation
where you feel that you cannot
cope, always remember RESCUE
REMEDY. You can take it as often
as you like, alongside homeopathic
remedies if you wish.

GRIEF

IGNATIA is the number-one remedy
for acute feelings of sadness and
loss. It can calm both the hysterical and over-sensitive and those
who keep their grief bottled up.

Above: A Pasque flower, used in Pulsatilla.

Above: Aconite.

Children and emotionally dependent people can be helped by *PULSATILLA*.

FRIGHT
ACONITE is the major remedy for helping people get over a shock or a terrifying experience.

ANTICIPATION
The worry over a forthcoming event such as an exam, appearing on the stage or meeting someone new can be very upsetting to some people. There are a number of remedies that can ease the anxiety and panic.

GELSEMIUM is best used when you start trembling with nerves and literally go weak at the knees. *ARG NIT* is a good all-round anxiety remedy, where there are symptoms of great restlessness. It also has a claustrophobic picture so could help with fear of flying or travelling by underground (subway). The panic often causes diarrhoea. Another anxiety remedy that can also affect the bowels is *LYCOPODIUM*. Strangely, people who need Lycopodium often excel at the ordeals they have been worrying about, once they have gone through the panic barrier.

INSOMNIA
There can be many causes of sleeplessness: worry, habit, bad eating patterns and others. For the "hamster on the wheel" syndrome, where your mind is rushing around in never-ending circles, *VALERIAN* can be magical. For constant early waking, especially if you live too much on your nerves and eat too much rich food, try *NUX VOMICA*.

Above: The herb Valerian, used in the remedy Valeriana.

REMEDIES: THE MATERIA MEDICA

There are perhaps 2,000 remedies in the homeopathic Materia Medica, as it is called, although most of them are best left to the practitioner.

However, there are a number of remedies that can be safely used by a lay person in low potencies for acute and first-aid purposes. The 42 remedies described in this chapter should be sufficient to cover most common problems.

Use this section to back up and confirm your choice from the remedies recommended for ailments in the previous chapter. If your choice still looks good, then you are probably on the right track. If it doesn't, consider one of the other remedies described for the ailment. Not every symptom of the remedy has to be present. Homeopaths

use the expression "a three-legged stool": if the remedy covers three symptoms of the condition, then it is likely to be well indicated.

Above: Calendula flowers.

Right: A selection of materials that make up traditional homeopathic remedies. Clockwise from left: magnesium phosphate, flowers of sulphur, ground oyster shells, natural sponge, raw potash, potassium dichromate, viburnum opulus and iron phosphate.

ACONITE

ACONITUM NAPELLUS

Monkshood, a beautiful yet poisonous plant with blue flowers, is native to mountainous areas of Europe and Asia. It is widely cultivated as a garden plant.

KEYNOTES
• Symptoms appear suddenly and violently, often at night.
• They may appear after catching a chill or after a fright.
• Fear or extreme anxiety may accompany symptoms.
• An important remedy for high fevers with extreme thirst and sweat.
• Major remedy for violent, dry croupy coughs.
• Best used at the beginning of an illness.

ALLIUM CEPA

ALLIUM CEPA

The remedy comes from the onion, whose characteristics are well known to anyone who has ever peeled one: it affects the mucous membranes of the nose, eyes and throat.

KEYNOTES
• Sneezing, often repeatedly, with a streaming nose.
• The nose and eyes burn and are irritated.
• Nasal discharge is acrid while the tears are bland.
• Major remedy for hay fever (when the nose is affected more than the eyes) and for colds.

ANT TART

ANTIMONIUM TARTARICUM

Ant tart is prepared from the chemical substance antimony potassium tartrate, traditionally known as tartar emetic. It affects the mucous membranes of the lungs.

KEYNOTES
• A wet, rattling cough from deep in the lungs, with shortness of breath and wheezing.
• Helps to bring up mucus from the lungs.

APIS

APIS MELLIFICA

The remedy is prepared from the honey-bee. The well-known effects of its sting describe the remedy picture very well.

KEYNOTES
• A useful remedy after injuries, especially from bites or stings where there is swelling, puffiness and redness.
• The affected area feels like a water bag.
• Fever appears quickly and without thirst.
• The person is restless and irritable.
• The symptoms are often relieved by cool air or cold compresses.

ARG NIT

ARGENTUM NITRICUM

Silver nitrate, from which this remedy is derived, is one of the silver compounds used in the photographic process. It helps to soothe an agitated nervous system.

KEYNOTES
• Panic, nervousness and anxiety.
• Feeling worried, hurried and unsupported.
• Fears of anticipation, such as stage fright, exams, visiting the dentist, flying and many others.
• The nervousness may cause diarrhoea and wind (gas).

ARNICA

ARNICA MONTANA

Arnica is a well-known herb with yellow, daisy-like flowers. It prefers to grow in mountainous areas. It has a special affinity with soft tissue and muscles, and is usually the first remedy to think of after any accident. Where there is bruising but the skin is not broken, use Arnica cream. (When the skin is broken, use Calendula or Hypercal cream instead.)

KEYNOTES
• The most important remedy for bruising.
• Shock following an accident.
• Muscle strains after strenuous or extreme exertion.

ARSENICUM

ARSENICUM ALBUM

Arsenic oxide is a well-known poison. However, used as a home-opathic remedy it is extremely safe and works especially well on the gastro-intestinal and respiratory systems.

KEYNOTES
• Vomiting, diarrhoea, abdominal and stomach cramps.
• It is often the first remedy to try for food poisoning.
• Asthmatic, wheezy breathing, often worse at night. Head colds with a runny nose.
• Chilliness, restlessness, anxiety and weakness accompany the other symptoms.
• Warmth gives great relief in most ailments.

BELLADONNA

ATROPA BELLADONNA

The remedy Belladonna is pre-pared from deadly nightshade, whose poisonous berries are best avoided. However, they produce a wonderful medicine which is one of the most important fever and headache remedies.

KEYNOTES
• Violent and intense symptoms appearing suddenly.
• Fever with high temperature, little thirst and burning, dry skin.
• The face or the affected part is usually bright red.
• Throbbing pains, especially in the head area.
• The pupils may be dilated and over-sensitive to light.

BRYONIA

BRYONIA ALBA

Bryonia is prepared from the roots of white bryony, a climbing plant found in hedgerows throughout Europe. The roots are enormous and store a great deal of water. Bryonia patients seem to lack "lubrication".

KEYNOTES
• The symptoms tend to develop slowly.
• Dryness marks all symptoms: in the mouth, membranes and joints.
• Extreme thirst.
• The condition feels worse for the slightest motion and better for firm pressure.
• Bryonia coughs are dry and very painful.
• The person is irritable.

CALENDULA

CALENDULA OFFICINALIS

Calendula has long been known to herbalists as a major first-aid remedy for injuries. It is prepared from the common marigold, and the simplest way to use it is as a cream. Sometimes it is combined with Hypericum and the combination is known as Hypercal. You can use this cream on all cuts, sores and open wounds. (For bruises where the skin is not broken, use Arnica cream.)

Calendula is a natural antiseptic and keeps the injury free of infection, as well as speeding up the healing process.

IPECAC

CEPHAELIS IPECACUANHA

Ipecacuanha is a small South American shrub. The remedy works mainly on the digestive and respiratory tracts and the outstanding symptom is nausea, whatever the ailment.

KEYNOTES
• Persistent nausea, not helped by vomiting.
• Coughs accompanied by nausea.
• Morning sickness in pregnancy.
• Asthma or wheeziness with nausea.
• "Sick" headaches.

COCCULUS

COCCULUS ORBICULATUS

The remedy is prepared from the Indian cockle, a plant that grows along the coasts of India. It profoundly affects the nervous system and can strengthen a weakened and exhausted system. Because it can also cure nausea and dizziness, it is an important remedy for travel sickness, whether on a boat, plane or in a car.

KEYNOTES
• Nausea, vomiting, and dizziness, as in travel sickness.
• Exhaustion and nervous stress, perhaps due to lack of sleep.

DROSERA

DROSERA ROTUNDIFOLIA

Drosera is a remedy prepared from an extraordinary insectivorous plant, the round-leaved sundew. Drosera affects the respiratory system and is an important cough remedy.

KEYNOTES
• Deep, barking coughs.
• Prolonged and incessant coughs returning in periodic fits or spasms.
• The cough may be so severe that it results in retching or vomiting.

EUPATORIUM

EUPATORIUM PERFOLIATUM

Eupatorium is a North American herb found growing in marshy places. Its common name, boneset, gives a clue to its use. Whatever the other symptoms, the bones usually ache. It is largely used as a flu remedy.

KEYNOTES
• Flu-like symptoms, with aching all over, but pains that seem to have lodged deep in the bones.
• There may be a painful cough, sometimes with nausea.

EUPHRASIA

EUPHRASIA OFFICINALIS

Also known as eyebright, Euphrasia has long been known as a remedy with a specific application to the eyes. It is a very pretty little meadow plant with colourful flowers that open wide only in sunshine.

KEYNOTES
• Eyes that are sore, red and inflamed.
• The eyes water with burning tears.
• In cases of hay fever, the symptoms are sneezing, itching and a runny nose, but the eyes are most affected.

FERRUM PHOS

FERRUM PHOSPHORICUM

Iron phosphate, from which Ferrum phos is prepared, is a mineral that balances the iron and oxygen in the blood. It is a tissue salt that can be used as a tonic in weak anaemic patients.

KEYNOTES
• Flu and cold symptoms that are not well defined.
• Weakness and tiredness.
• General anaemia: the remedy can be very useful for women with heavy periods or during a pregnancy.

GELSEMIUM

GELSEMIUM SEMPERVIRENS

The remedy is prepared from a North American plant known as yellow jasmine. It acts specifically on the muscles, motor nerves and nervous system, and is probably the most important acute remedy for flu.

KEYNOTES
• Aching, heavy muscles which will not obey the will.
• Tiredness, weakness, shivering and trembling.
• Fever with sweating but little thirst.
• Headaches concentrated at the back of the head.
• Anticipation: the muscles tremble with fear at the thought of, or during, an ordeal.

HEPAR SULPH

HEPAR SULPHURIS CALCAREUM

The remedy was developed by Hahnemann himself from calcium sulphide, which is made by heating flowers of sulphur and the lime of oyster shells together. It strongly affects the nervous system and is good in acute septic states (infected areas) and in respiratory system problems.

KEYNOTES
• Extreme irritability and over-sensitivity.
• Coldness, especially around the head.
• Hoarse, dry coughs with yellow mucus, croup.
• Abscesses and boils that contain a lot of pus and are slow to heal.
• Heavy perspiration.

HYPERICUM

HYPERICUM PERFORATUM

Prepared from the herb St John's Wort, Hypericum is primarily an injury remedy working particularly on areas rich in sensitive nerves: fingers, toes, lips, ears, eyes, and the coccyx at the base of the spine. Use Hypericum instead of Arnica for bruising in such sensitive areas, although Arnica may also work well.

KEYNOTE
• Pains are often felt shooting up the limbs, along the tracks of the nerves.

IGNATIA

IGNATIA AMARA

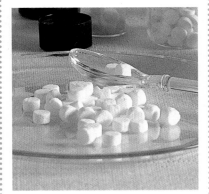

Ignatia is prepared from the seeds of a tree, the St Ignatius bean, which grows in South East Asia. It is a major "grief" remedy and strongly affects the emotions.

KEYNOTES
• Sadness and grief following emotional loss.
• Changeable moods: tears following laughter, or hysteria.
• Suppressed emotions, when the tears won't come.
• Pronounced sighing following a period of anxiety, fear or grief.

KALI BICH

KALI BICHROMICUM

The source of Kali bichromicum, potassium dichromate, is a chemical compound involved in many industrial processes, such as dyeing, printing and photography. It especially affects the mucous membranes of the air passages and is an important sinusitis remedy.

KEYNOTES
• Thick, strong, lumpy green discharges from the nasal passages or mouth.
• Headaches in small spots as a result of catarrh.
• Dry cough with sticky, yellow-green mucus.

LACHESIS

LACHESIS MUTA

Lachesis is prepared from the venom of the bushmaster snake native to South America. Generally it is a chronic remedy best left in the hands of professional homeopaths, but it does have an acute use in treating sore throats and menstrual problems.

KEYNOTES
• Sore throats, much worse on the left side.
• Painful throats where liquids are more difficult to swallow than solids.
• Menstrual pains and tension improve when the flow starts.
• Hot flushes around the time of the menopause.

LEDUM

LEDUM PALUSTRE

The small shrub known as marsh tea from which Ledum is derived grows in boggy places across the cold wastes of the Northern Hemisphere. It is primarily a first-aid injury remedy, where cold rather than warmth is found to be soothing.

KEYNOTES
• Puncture wounds such as from nails or splinters, bites and stings, whose pain is eased by cold compresses.
• Wounds that look puffy and feel cold.
• Injuries to the eye, which looks cold, puffy and bloodshot.

LYCOPODIUM

LYCOPODIUM CLAVATUM

This remedy is prepared from the spores of club moss, a strange prostrate plant which likes to grow on heaths. It is mainly prescribed constitutionally for chronic conditions but it can be very helpful for digestive problems and sometimes for acute sore throats.

KEYNOTES
• Conditions that are worse on the right side or that move from the right to the left side of the body.
• Flatulence and pain in the abdomen or stomach.
• The problem is aggravated by gassy foods such as beans.
• The person may crave sweet things to eat.

CANTHARIS

LYTTA VESICATORIA

Cantharis is one of a few homeo-pathic remedies prepared from insects. It is derived from an iri-descent green beetle commonly called Spanish fly. It is also known as the blister beetle, as it is a major irritant if handled. It has an affini-ty with the urinary tract.

KEYNOTES
• Cystitis - where there are intense, burning pains on urinating.
• Burns or burning pains generally, such as in sunburn or burns from hot pans.

MAG PHOS

MAGNESIA PHOSPHORICA

Magnesia phosphorica is one of the 12 tissue salts, as well as being a remedy, and works directly in easing tension in the nerves and muscles. It can therefore be an effective painkiller.

KEYNOTES
• Violent, cramping, spasmodic pains, often in the abdominal area.
• Pains are better for warmth, gentle massage or doubling up.
• Can help with colic, period pains, sciatica, toothache or earache.

CHAMOMILLA

MATRICARIA CHAMOMILLA

Chamomile is a member of the daisy family and grows wild throughout Europe and the US. It strongly affects the nervous system. The remedy is considered one of the most important medicines for the treatment of children: Aconite, Belladonna and Chamomilla are together known as the "ABC" remedies.

KEYNOTES
• Bad temper and irritability.
• Teething problems in angry babies.
• In cases of colic, the stools are usually offensive, slimy and green.
• Extreme sensitivity to pain.
• The child's temper is worse for being looked at or spoken to, and better for being rocked or carried.

MERCURIUS

MERCURIUS SOLUBILIS

The name of this remedy is sometimes abbreviated to Merc sol. It is prepared from the liquid metal mercury. It is used in acute septic states (infected areas) where the glands and their secretions are particularly affected.

KEYNOTES
• Swollen and tender glands.
• Profuse sweating and increased thirst.
• The breath, sweat and secretions are usually offensive.
• The tongue looks flabby, yellow and coated.
• Fevers blow hot and cold.
• Irritability and restlessness.

PHOSPHORUS

PHOSPHORUS

The element phosphorus is an important constituent of the body, particularly of the bones. It is normally used as a major constitutional remedy, but can be useful in some acute situations. These include digestive problems, with immediate vomiting once the food has warmed in the stomach, and constant diarrhoea as if a tap has been turned on. Phosphorus can also help with minor haemorrhages such as nosebleeds. A very useful application is for the "spacey" feeling that lingers too long after an anaesthetic.

KEYNOTE
• Suits people who are lively, open and friendly, but who are also occasionally nervous and anxious.

PHYTOLACCA

PHYTOLACCA DECANDRA

Phytolacca or poke-root is a plant that grows across the northern hemisphere. It is a glandular remedy that particularly affects the tonsils and mammary glands. Phytolacca is probably the most important remedy for mastitis.

KEYNOTES
• Sore throats that look dark and angry.
• Sore throats in which the pain feels like a hot ball and may extend to the ears.
• Swollen, tender breasts with hard lumps and cracked nipples.

PULSATILLA

PULSATILLA NIGRICANS

Pulsatilla is one of the most useful of acute remedies, as well as being a very important constitutional one. The remedy comes from the pasque flower and is also known as the weathercock remedy because it suits people whose moods and symptoms are constantly changing. For this reason, it is a wonderful remedy for small children.

KEYNOTES
• Tendency to be weepy and clingy, feeling unsupported.
• Suits people with gentle, sympathetic natures.
• Yellow-green discharge from the eyes or nose.
• Symptoms are helped by sympathy and fresh cool air.

RHUS TOX

RHUS TOXICODENDRON

The remedy is prepared from poison ivy, native to North America. Its main use is in sprains, strains and swollen joints, but because of its itchy, rashy picture it can be a good remedy for illnesses such as chickenpox or shingles. It is also a useful remedy for acute rheumatism.

KEYNOTES
• Extreme restlessness with a red, itchy rash.
• Stiffness in the joints, which is eased by gentle motion.
• The symptoms are better for warmth and worse for cold, damp and over-exertion.

RUTA

RUTA GRAVEOLENS

Ruta, or rue, is an ancient herbal remedy that has been called the herb of grace. It acts particularly on the joints, tendons, cartilages and periosteum (the membrane that covers the bones). It also has an affinity with the eyes.

KEYNOTES
• Bruises to the bones.
• Strains to the joints and connecting tissue, especially to the ankles and wrists.
• The symptoms are worse for cold and damp and better for warmth.
• Eye strain, with dim vision, from overwork.

SEPIA

SEPIA OFFICINALIS

Sepia is a remedy prepared from the ink of the squid or cuttlefish. Normally its use should be left to the professional homeopath as it has a "big" picture (i.e. can be used in many circumstances), but because of its affinity with the female reproductive system it can be helpful in some menstrual problems.

KEYNOTES
• Suits tired, depressed, emotionally withdrawn people.
• Morning sickness in pregnancy, which is worse for the smell of food.
• Hot flushes during the menopause.
• Exercise may relieve the mental and emotional symptoms.

SILICA

SILICEA

Silica is a mineral derived from flint. It is one of the 12 tissue salts, and its presence in the body aids the elimination of toxins. It can be used acutely in septic (infected) conditions to strengthen the body's resistance to continual infection and help to expel foreign bodies such as splinters. Silica can also help to bring lingering abscesses or boils to a head, or help the body to re-absorb pus harmlessly if appropriate.

KEYNOTES
• Suitable for symptoms that are slow to heal, or for people who feel the cold, or who lack stamina or vitality.
• Small-scale infections that seem to be turning septic or putrid, rather than healing.

SPONGIA

SPONGIA TOSTA

Spongia, as its name indicates, is a remedy prepared from the lightly roasted skeleton of the marine sponge. It works very well on the respiratory tract and is one of homeopathy's major cough remedies, and an important croup remedy for children.

KEYNOTES
• Dry spasmodic cough.
• The cough sounds like a saw being pulled through wood.

NUX VOMICA

STRYCHNOS NUX VOMICA

Nux vomica is prepared from the seeds of the poison nut tree of Southeast Asia. It is a remedy that has many uses in both chronic and acute situations, and is especially useful when the digestive system is involved.

KEYNOTES
• Nausea or vomiting after a rich meal, when the food remains undigested like a load in the stomach.
• A feeling that if only you could vomit you would feel better.
• An urge to pass a stool – but the results are unsatisfying.
• Heartburn with a feeling of sourness.
• Hangover headaches.

SYMPHYTUM

SYMPHYTUM OFFICINALE

The remedy is prepared from the common herb comfrey. It is also known as knitbone, which indicates its main use in promoting the healing of broken bones. Use the remedy daily for several weeks after the bone has been set. Symphytum can also be used for injuries to the eyeball, such as after receiving the full force of a tennis ball directly in the eye.

KEYNOTES
• Speeds up the knitting or fusing together of bones.
• Injuries to the eyeball, such as being hit by a hard object.

VALERIAN

VALERIANA OFFICINALIS

Valerian is a well-known herb whose overuse in the 19th century caused insomnia and overtaxation of the nervous system to the point of hysteria. Because of the principle "like cures like", very tiny doses such as those used in homeopathy can cure these very same problems. Valerian is an important remedy for sleeplessness. Take one pill about an hour before bedtime.

KEYNOTE
• Especially useful when the mind feels like a "hamster on a wheel".

VERBASCUM
VERBASCUM THAPSUS

Verbascum is prepared from the great mullein, a common wayside herb. Its special use is in earaches, and it is best used as an oil. The remedy is especially helpful for children, who tend to suffer from ear infections more often than adults. Place a few drops of the oil in a warmed teaspoon and gently insert into the ear, with the child lying on one side.

KEYNOTE
• Earaches of all kinds, both in children and adults.

VIBURNUM OPULUS
VIBURNUM OPULUS

The guelder rose is widely distributed in woods and damp places throughout northern Europe and the US. It is also known as cramp bark and the homeopathic remedy, which is prepared from the bark, can be very helpful for period pains and spasmodic cramps.

KEYNOTE
• For severe cramping and muscle spasms.

RESCUE REMEDY

Although not strictly a homeopathic remedy – it is a combination of five of the Bach Flower essences – Rescue Remedy is such a wonderful medicine to have in your first-aid kit, it would be a real hardship to do without it. It usually comes in the form of a tincture, although it can also be bought as a cream. In any extreme crisis or shock, whether mental, emotional or physical, place a few drops on the tongue as often as necessary. Rescue Remedy can safely be used in conjunction with homeopathic remedies, or with other treatments or medicines.

THE POWER OF PLANTS: *the Art of Herbalism*

USE THE VARIOUS properties of beneficial herbs to help you feel more healthy and better able to cope with everyday problems. Very simple remedies can be made easily from dried or fresh herbs, and substituting herbal teas for stimulating drinks such as tea, coffee and cola will help you to relax and reduce tension. There is much you can do with herbs yourself to treat minor health problems and help your body deal with everyday stresses.

PLANTING A HERB GARDEN

You don't need very much space to grow herbs: a small border, or even a collection of containers, will provide an adequate supply. If you do have the room, of course, a full-scale herb garden is not only practical but rewarding and decorative as well.

SOIL AND SITE

Most herbs are undemanding and easy to grow. They are essentially wild plants, and do not require rich, highly cultivated soil. Many of the most useful herbs, such as Sage, Thyme, Rosemary and Lavender, are Mediterranean natives and will not stand heavy clay soils or water-logged conditions. Even naturally moisture-loving plants, such as Lemon Balm, Mint and Valerian, will grow happily in a light soil, though not in conditions of total drought. A sunny, sheltered position protected from biting winter winds will suit the plants, though some such as Lemon Verbena and Bay may need winter protection.

▶ A formal framework of rectangular beds and gravel paths keeps herbs neatly under control and makes cultivating and picking much easier.

DESIGN

A formal layout of small beds dissected by paths provides a satisfying framework for the lax, untidy growth of many herbs. It also makes tending and harvesting the plants easier. A single species to each bed can look really effective, evoking the style of medieval herb gardens. In complete contrast, an informal cottage-garden style provides plenty of scope for imaginative, exuberant planting. Raised beds or large containers make easy-to-control, self-contained herb gardens.

▲ Lemon Balm grows prolifically and needs trimming regularly.

MAINTENANCE

Many herbs are prolific growers. Harvesting helps to keep them under control, but don't be afraid to cut them back ruthlessly. A light mulch of garden compost, applied in spring or autumn, helps to keep the herbs in good heart. Most of the plants will stand dry summers, but moisture-lovers such as Mint and Valerian, which are apt to bolt if it is too dry, will need watering.

▲ Lavender makes a scented and sturdy hedge in a herb garden.

▶ (clockwise from front): Thyme, Golden Marjoram and Rue.

PREPARING HERBS

If you grow herbs in your garden they can be used fresh (except Pasque Flower), or harvested when they are abundant and dried for future use. Simple herbal remedies can be made up for use either internally or externally. Many herbs are, of course, a delicious addition to food, or they can be taken internally in a variety of other forms: as teas, decoctions, tinctures, inhalations, capsules and powders.

Relaxing herbs such as Hops and Lavender can be combined in a sleep pillow.

Externally, herbs can be applied as compresses, poultices, ointments, creams or infused oils. You can also add fresh herbs or herbal oils to your bath for a therapeutic soak.

Essential oils, fluid extracts and tablets are usually produced industrially and are not suitable for making at home.

Facing page: Simple herbal remedies can be made easily and cheaply using everyday kitchen equipment.

Herbal preparations need to be stored in airtight containers. Dark glass is best for long-term storage of tinctures and oils.

Teas from fresh and dried herbs can be made in a tea pot or cafetière.

CAUTION
- Avoid all strong herbal teas during the first three months of pregnancy.
- Do not give Peppermint or Sage tea to children under four years of age.
- Avoid ready-made herbal mixes that contain sugar.

GATHERING AND STORING HERBS

Identifying, growing and harvesting herbs can be a healing experience in itself. Handling herbs will bring you closer to nature and increase your appreciation of the amazing vitality of plants.

GROWING

The best way to acquire herbs to help you keep well is of course to grow them yourself. This way you can be sure of what they are and that they are healthy, organically grown and fresh. Most of the herbs used in the remedies in this book will grow well in temperate climates. Many are usually considered to be weeds and actually thrive on disturbed ground and with little care. They bring a sense of vitality to a garden and being among them and harvesting them is enlivening.

GATHERING

The aerial parts of herbs (the flowers, stems and leaves) should be gathered for use or for drying when the plants are in bud and totally dry. Roots should be dug in the autumn, cleaned and chopped into small pieces.

If you harvest from the wild, make quite sure that you have identified the plant correctly (use a good wild flower book) and that it is not polluted by fertilizers, pesticides or car emissions. Never pick so much that you reduce next year's growth.

Many of the herbs found in gardens today have been used by herbalists for over two thousand years.

Lime Blossom is abundant for easy picking in both the countryside and urban areas during early summer.

Freshly picked Lime Blossom ready for drying or for using fresh to make a tea or tincture.

DRYING

Spread your herbs out to dry naturally in an airy position out of direct sunlight. The surroundings should be very dry. Small quantities can be dried effectively in loosely sealed paper bags.

St. John's Wort dries very well. Spread the stems out evenly to dry and avoid them touching each other.

Herbs dry well when hanging in a dry, airy place, which is out of direct sunlight.

STORING

Store dried herbs in separate, airtight containers away from the light. Don't forget to label and date them. They will keep for up to six months.

Instead of drying your herbs, you can store them in the freezer. This is especially useful for herbs such as Lemon Balm and Parsley, which lose their flavour when they are dried.

BUYING

Many shops stock dried herbs. Buy these only if they seem fresh – they should be brightly coloured and strongly aromatic.

Some herbal remedies are now readily available over the counter in the form of capsules, tablets or tinctures. These are usually of good quality. Choose the simpler ones that tell you exactly the type and quantity of herb involved.

MAKING TEAS

Herbal teas are also called infusions or tisanes, and are a simple and delicious way of extracting the goodness and flavour from the aerial parts of herbs. You can use either fresh or dried herbs to make a tea (use twice as much fresh plant material as dried). If you find the taste of some herb teas bitter, they can be sweetened with a little honey or flavoured by stirring with a Licorice stick or adding slices of fresh Ginger.

1 Put your chosen herb or herbs into a pot or cup. A standard-strength tea is made with 1 tsp dried or 2 tsp fresh herb to each cup of water.

2 Add boiling water, cover with a lid and leave to steep for 10–15 minutes.

3 Strain and drink as required. Teas can be drunk hot or cold. They can be re-heated.

Left: Teas will keep in the fridge in a covered container for up to 24 hours.

Right: Herb teas can also be made in a cafetière. Simply fill the cafetière with the fresh or dried herbs and add boiling water. Allow to steep for 10-15 minutes before pressing down the plunger.

MAKING DECOCTIONS

Infusing in boiling water is not enough to extract the constituents from roots or bark. This harder plant material needs to be boiled and the resulting liquid is called a decoction. Use a stainless steel, glass or enamelled pan, not aluminium, to prepare decoctions.

1 Roots and barks need to be harvested in the autumn and prepared for use.

2 Trim the aerial parts of the plant away from the root.

3 Wash the roots thoroughly in clean water, then chop into small pieces.

4 Fill a pan with cold water and add 1 tsp of the chopped herb material per cup of water. Bring to the boil and simmer for 10–15 minutes.

5 Strain off the liquid and allow to cool before drinking. Decoctions, like teas, can be kept for 24 hours in the fridge. They can be drunk hot or cold.

NERVINES SUITABLE FOR DECOCTIONS
- Valerian
- Licorice
- Cramp Bark

Avoid Licorice if you have high blood pressure.

MAKING TINCTURES

Sometimes it is more convenient to take a spoonful of medicine rather than make a tea or decoction. Tinctures are made by steeping herbs in a mixture of alcohol and water. The alcohol extracts the medicinal constituents and also acts as a preservative.

1 Place 100 g/4 oz dried herbs or 300 g/11 oz fresh herbs in a jar.

2 Add 250 ml/8 fl oz/1 cup vodka and 250 ml/8 fl oz/1 cup water.

3 Leave the herbs to steep in the liquid for a month, preferably on a sunny windowsill. Gently shake the jar daily.

4 Strain and store the tincture in a dark glass bottle (it will keep up to 18 months).

MAKING SYRUPS

Herb syrups make good remedies for giving to children. They also improve the flavour of bitter herbs such as Motherwort and Vervain.

1 Place 500 g/1¼ lb sugar or honey in a pan and add 1 litre/ 1¾ pints/4 cups water.
2 Heat gently, stirring, to dissolve the sugar or honey.
3 Add 150 g/5 oz plant material and heat gently for 5 minutes.
4 Turn off the heat and allow to steep overnight.
5 Strain and store in an airtight container for future use. The sugar acts as a preservative so a herb syrup will keep for 18 months.

COLD INFUSED OILS

Herbal oils are suitable for external use in massage, as bath oils or for conditioning the hair and skin. Cold infused oils are simple to prepare and are an effective way to infuse delicate flowerheads such as St. John's Wort and Chamomile.

1 Fill a glass storage jar with the flowers or leaves of your chosen dried herb.

2 Pour in a light vegetable oil to cover the herbs – try sunflower or grape seed oil.

3 Allow the jar to stand on a sunny windowsill for a month to steep. Give it a shake every day.

4 Strain the flowers or leaves. For a stronger infusion, renew the herbs in the oil every two weeks.

5 Pour into stoppered bottles to store.

USEFUL HERBS FOR MAKING INFUSED OILS
- Rosemary
- Lavender
- St. John's Wort
- Chamomile
- Marjoram

Do not put St. John's Wort oil on the skin before going into bright sunshine.

HERBS AND FOOD

Plants are very nutritious. They are our main source of vitamins and minerals and provide carbohydrate, protein and roughage. The plants usually called herbs are particularly potent. This points out the narrow divide between food and medicine – a well-nourished body is less likely to get ill. Nettle, for example, contains iron and vitamin C. Kelp contains sodium, potassium, calcium, magnesium, iron, zinc, copper, aluminium and silica as well as vitamin B1 (thiamin). Alfalfa also makes a good multivitamin and mineral supplement since it contains all the vitamins as well as calcium, magnesium, phosphorus and potassium.

Culinary herbs improve digestion and general health as well as tasting delicious.

Knowing about the nutritional value of herbs can change your attitude to cooking: adding generous portions of herbs to food becomes more than just adding flavour. Herbs can also be added fresh to salads as a pleasurable way of avoiding nutritional deficiencies.

The wild plants from which some cultivated vegetables were developed are still useful to herbalists. Wild Carrot *(Daucus carota)* is a common hedgerow plant used for urinary problems and to improve digestion. Wild Lettuce *(Lactuca virosa)* is a mild sedative and painkiller used to irritable reduce coughs and restlessness.

Not only is what you eat important, but the efficiency with which food is absorbed is crucial. Many herbs stimulate digestive enzymes and encourage efficient intestinal activity. Some of these are still used as culinary herbs: Fennel, Caraway, Dill and Cumin all contain antispasmodic oils which reduce colic. Bitter herbs such as Dandelion encourage liver function. Others, such as Senna, encourage bowel activity.

Experiment with herbs in food. *A Modern Herbal* by Maud Grieve (1931) is a fascinating source of information and contains many old recipes.

Many of the culinary herbs we use today were distributed throughout Europe by the Roman army.

GUIDE TO HERBS AND THEIR USES

The herbs described on the following pages are particularly useful for managing stress and other common conditions. Reading about them and studying the pictures will help you to decide which would be most beneficial for you. You may want to try several before deciding which you find most helpful. Herbs do not usually work instantly, so give them at least two weeks to begin to take effect. If you do not feel better in three weeks, seek the help of a qualified practitioner. Herbs can be used in various combinations, and you will find suggestions for putting them together to give additional benefits.

Most of us would benefit from a nerve tonic during stressful times of our lives. Select a herbal remedy which best suits your symptoms. For example, if when under stress you start to feel depressed you should look for a stimulating herbal tonic such as Wild Oats. If, however, stress makes you anxious with symptoms such as palpitations, sweating and sleeplessness, turn towards relaxing herbs.

A selection of herbs useful in managing stress and other conditions.

Above: Correct identification is very important. *Hypericum perforatum* is the only St. John's Wort with oil glands in the leaves. The glands look like tiny holes when held towards the light.
Facing page: Lavender is grown in Europe for its essential oils.

CHAMOMILE

GERMAN CHAMOMILE *CHAMOMILLA RECUTITA* OR ROMAN CHAMOMILE *CHAMAEMELUM NOBILE*

This pretty little daisy is one of the better known herbs, possibly because it is so useful. Its nature is friendly and supportive, both to people and to other plants. It has been called "the plants' physician" because other species growing near it seem to thrive. Use the flowerheads alone in a tea or tincture to relax both the digestive function and those gut feelings which may sometimes disturb you. It makes a very suitable tea to drink late in the day, as it has quite the opposite effect to that of coffee, which exacerbates tension and anxiety.

Known as "mother of the gut", Chamomile reduces spasm and inflammation in the digestive system at the same time as it improves liver function by its bitter action. This makes it an ideal after-dinner drink, especially as it also promotes relaxation. Many people swear by Chamomile tea as the ideal bedtime

Dried Chamomile flowers.

Chamomile is a member of the daisy family.

drink. This gentle plant can also be used to soothe restless babies and children.

Chamomile tea bags are useful and convenient but an infusion of loose flowers usually makes a better quality tea. Be sure that those you buy are fresh: they should be recognizable flowerheads, bright yellow and white. Inhaling the steam from a cup of Chamomile tea reduces the effects of nasal irritants and will soothe the symptoms of hay fever or allergic rhinitis. Tea bags can also be added to the bath to encourage relaxation.
PARTS USED Flowerheads.
DOSE 1tsp dried/2 tsp fresh to a cup of boiling water.

LEMON BALM

MELISSA OFFICINALIS, BEE BALM

This plant has so much vitality that it can spread all over the garden. Also called Bee Balm, it is so much enjoyed by bees that it has been suggested that hives rubbed with the plant will keep the bees close and encourage others to join the hives.

With its lemon-honey scent and tiny white flowers, Lemon Balm makes a suitable drink for every day, hot in the winter and iced in the summer. This is one of the few herbs which doesn't keep its flavour on drying, so if you have a garden you would be well advised to pick it fresh daily – a constructive way to restrain its rampant habit! If you want to use it in the winter, the best solution is to freeze it. Pick it in early summer when abundant, and freeze it in a plastic container.

Lemon Balm supports digestion and relaxation, and is helpful for sensitive digestive systems. It is much used for irritable bowel, nervous indigestion, anxiety and depression. Drinking Lemon Balm tea also encourages a clear head, so it is useful when you are studying. It makes a good bedtime drink, promoting peaceful sleep and relaxation.

Lemon Balm combines well with Chamomile.

PARTS USED Leaves and flowers.

DOSE 1 tsp to a cup of boiling water, up to 3-4 times a day.

Lemon Balm helps reduce agitation caused by stress.

WOOD BETONY

STACHYS BETONICA syn. *S. OFFICINALIS, BETONICA OFFICINALIS,* BISHOP'S WEED

An attractive plant with purple flowers growing out of a satisfying cushion of leaves, Wood Betony restores the nervous system, especially if sick headaches and poor memory are a problem. It has the effect of encouraging blood flow to the head.

It has always been a very popular remedy throughout Europe and is also called Bishop's Weed, perhaps because it was often planted on holy ground. A wide range of beneficial qualities have been ascribed to Wood Betony and it is certainly worth trying if you are troubled with headaches or migraines.

PARTS USED Aerial parts.

DOSE 1tsp dried/2 tsp fresh herb to a cup of boiling water.

CAUTION
Avoid high doses in pregnancy.

The flowers of Wood Betony appear in midsummer.

SKULLCAP

SCUTELLARIA LATERIFLORA

This herb is another nervous tonic. It was traditionally associated with the head, because it produces skull-like seed pods. It is very calming, having the same effect as a gentle hand placed on the head. Skullcap can help the anxiety and restlessness which often accompany an overload of worries or responsibilities. Its bitter taste encourages the liver to remove toxins from the body; this includes excess hormones which are often responsible for premenstrual tension.

PARTS USED Aerial parts, harvested after flowering.

DOSE 1 tsp dried/2 tsp fresh herb to a cup of boiling water.

Skullcap takes its name from the skull-like seed pods.

GINSENG

KOREAN GINSENG, *PANAX SPP.*

The name of this plant means "wonder of the world" By improving the production of adrenal hormones, Korean Ginseng helps the body to adapt to stress and resist disease. Because it is stimulating, prolonged use could be exhausting, but as a short-term remedy for fatigue or debility it is very effective.

In China, small doses are taken to support health in the elderly and to protect from serious disease. Korean Ginseng also has a reputation as an aphrodisiac and induces energy of every type. In the West it is usually prescribed during periods of particular stress or to those suffering from debilitating diseases such as ME.

SIBERIAN GINSENG, *ELEUTHEROCOCCUS SENTICOSUS*

Siberian Ginseng is a European plant which, like Korean Ginseng, improves the ability to adapt to stress. It is less stimulating, but increases stamina and skilled performance.

Both Korean and Siberian Ginseng improve clarity of mind and are helpful when preparing for exams or other demanding projects.

PARTS USED Dried root.

DOSE 1 g per day or as instructed for shorter periods.

CAUTION
• Avoid the use of Ginseng during pregnancy or with other stimulants.
• Do not take high doses for more than six weeks without expert advice.
• Stop taking Ginseng if it makes you feel agitated or you develop a headache.

Ginseng is a common over-the-counter remedy. Make sure it is of good quality – usually the more expensive brands are better.

LICORICE

Licorice is a member of the pea family.

Licorice sticks are sections of root. The black bars are made of solidified juice and are very strong.

GLYCYRRHIZA GLABRA

This is an extremely useful herb which has been cultivated since the Middle Ages for its sweet, aromatic roots. Among its many actions is its beneficial effect on digestion: it reduces inflammation all along the gut and encourages bowel activity – Licorice is the basis of most proprietory laxatives. It is often used as a flavouring and will not raise blood sugar levels. If you like it, add a little to sweeten any herb tea – just stand a stick in the cup until you achieve the sweetness you want. Under close supervision, the root can be given to babies to chew and will ease the pain of teething.

Licorice also supports the adrenal glands and is therefore useful in any inflammatory condition such as eczema or arthritis. It will help to restore natural steroid production after a course of steroid medication. Since stress requires the adrenal glands to keep producing adrenaline, it may be that people who love to eat Licorice daily are instinctively seeking support for stressful times or lifestyles.

Licorice heated in honey makes a soothing syrup, which helps to relax the chest in conditions such as bronchitis and asthma.

PARTS USED The root (Licorice sticks) or solidified juice in the form of black bars.

DOSE 1 tsp to a cup of boiling water.

CAUTION
Licorice is not recommended for those with high blood pressure.

BORAGE

BORAGO OFFICINALIS

This strapping plant, with bristly and fleshy stems and leaves, sports surprisingly exotic, luminous blue flowers. These are traditionally used in drinks to raise the spirits. They make an attractive garnish to many dishes, especially ice cream and other cold summer puddings. Traditionally associated with courage, Borage improves the production of adrenaline and is therefore, like Licorice, useful during stressful times or after steroid medication.

This plant is very nutritious, containing calcium, potassium and traces of gamma linoleic acid. It also helps in the absorption of iron. Oil from the seeds is a good alternative to Evening Primrose oil in treating skin disease or rheumatism. It is commercially available in capsules and is sometimes called Starflower oil.

In addition to bringing "courage and good heart", Borage increases milk production in nursing mothers and is a useful herb to take during fevers, infections and convalescence.

PARTS USED Leaves, flowers and seeds. The leaves, being so fleshy, need to be dried quickly and are best heated very gently in a cool oven until crisp.

DOSE 1 tsp dried/2 tsp fresh to a cup of boiling water.

Borage is a rampant plant and seeds itself easily.

"Borage cheers the heart and raises drooping spirits."
DIOSCORIDES

HOPS

The twining stem of the fast-growing Hop vine.

Golden Hops are so called because of their brightly coloured leaves.

HUMULUS LUPULUS

The name Hop comes from the Anglo-Saxon *hoppen*, "to climb": the twining fibrous stems may reach some 4.5 m/15 ft in height. Like Hemp, fibre from the stems was at one time used to make coarse fabric and paper. Nowadays the plant is best-known for its use in brewing; beer made with Hops replaced traditional herb ales made from malt and cleared with Ground Ivy. Hops have the advantage of flavouring as well as clearing beer, but their introduction remained controversial for many years and Henry VIII forbade their use as they "spoiled the taste and endangered the people". Hops were thought to provoke melancholy and their use is still not advised for those who are feeling depressed. Hops are also known to reduce sexual potency.

Hops·are taken as a bitter tonic which improves digestion and reduces restlessness. It also has a sedative effect and will provoke deep sleep. The action is due, in part, to the presence of volatile oils, which give the characteristic odour and make pillows stuffed with dried Hops useful for restless sleepers.

The tender young shoots can be eaten raw or cooked and eaten like asparagus in the spring.

PARTS USED Dried flowers from the female plant, called "strobiles".

DOSE Not more than 1 tsp a day.

CAUTION
Avoid the use of Hops during depressive illness.

VALERIAN

VALERIANA OFFICINALIS, ALL HEAL

This Valerian is not the jolly red or white plant seen decorating walls (*Centranthus ruber*), but a tall herb with whitish-pink flowers which grows in damp places. When dried, the root has a characteristic earthy smell that attracts cats.

Valerian root has a powerful sedative effect on the nervous system and reduces tension and anxiety very effectively. It can be used to reduce hyperactivity, palpitations, spasm, period pain and tranquillizer withdrawal. It is especially useful if anxiety makes sleep difficult.

PARTS USED Dried root.

DOSE 1tsp to a cup of boiling water at bedtime.

CAUTION

High doses taken over a long period may cause headaches.

Valerian roots are harvested after the leaves have died.

Valerian grows in damp woods and meadows.

PASSIONFLOWER

PASSIFLORA INCARNATA, MAYPOP

This is a climbing plant which produces spectacular flowers and edible fruit. The species used medicinally prefers a warm, sunny climate. Buy it dried from a supplier to make sure you get the right plant.

Passionflower is often included in sleeping mixes and is very helpful for restlessness and insomnia. It seems to counteract the effects of adrenaline, thus reducing the "fight or flight" response which may cause anxiety, palpitations or nervous tremors.

It is also used as a painkiller to ease neuralgia and the pain of shingles.

PARTS USED Dried leaves and flowers.

DOSE ¼–½ tsp dried herb twice a day, or 1 tsp at night, or take an over-the-counter preparation as directed.

CALIFORNIAN POPPY

ESCHSCHOLZIA CALIFORNICA

The beautiful, delicate flowers last for only one day, then disappear to be replaced by long pointed seed pods. The stunning hot orange, yellow and pinkish colours of the blooms perhaps account for its French name, *globe de soleil*.

Californian Poppy is a gentle painkiller and sedative which reduces spasm and over-excitability. It combines well with Passionflower.

PARTS USED The whole plant, dried.

DOSE 1 tsp dried herb to a cup of boiling water.

CAUTION
Avoid this herb if you suffer from glaucoma.

Passionflower is said to resemble Christ's thorn crown.

The Californian Poppy thrives in sun and poor soil.

SAGE

SALVIA OFFICINALIS

A beautiful, evergreen plant with fine purple flowers in early summer, Sage looks strong and supportive. Like many culinary herbs, it aids digestion, while the familiar aroma recalls roast dinners.

It has antiseptic properties and can be used as a compress on wounds that are slow to heal or as a gargle or mouthwash for infections of the mouth or throat. It is also said that it will darken greying hair if used as a rinse.

Sage reduces secretions: it can be used to slow milk production during weaning and to reduce night sweats and menopausal hot flushes. During the menopause its beneficial action is supported by the slight oestrogen content of the herb.

For the nervous system, Culpeper described Sage as warming, improving the memory and quickening the senses. It is recommended for debility and confusion and has been associated with longevity.

PARTS USED Leaves and flowers.

Sage is currently being investigated as a possible remedy for Alzheimer's disease.

DOSE 1 tsp dried/2 tsp fresh to a cup of boiling water. If taking Sage regularly at therapeutic doses, take for three weeks then miss a week before continuing.

CAUTION
Avoid during pregnancy.

Sage can be toxic at high doses or over long periods.

MUGWORT

ARTEMISIA VULGARIS

Called the "mother of herbs", Mugwort has been considered a magical herb in many cultures. It grows robustly along roadsides and is said to protect the traveller. In some traditions, it was hung in the house or made into amulets to keep away evil spirits. Mugwort also repels insects, including moths.

This is a herb with many actions. Best described as a tonic with particular application to the digestive and nervous systems, it reduces nervous indigestion, nausea and irritability. As a womb tonic it is useful to regulate periods and reduce period pain and PMS. Fluff from the flowers is burnt as *moxa* in Chinese and Japanese medicine.

PARTS USED Flowers and leaves.

DOSE ¼–½ tsp three times a day.

CAUTION
Avoid in pregnancy.

Mugwort is a sturdy tonic herb which can grow up to 1 m/3 ft high.

The grey-green foliage of Mugwort shimmering at the roadside makes this a distinctive herb.

ST. JOHN'S WORT

HYPERICUM PERFORATUM

There are many plants in the St. John's Wort family, but only the wild *Hypericum perforatum* has the tiny oil glands which contain hypericin. To be sure that you have the right plant, hold up a leaf to the sun – the oil glands look like little holes, hence the name *perforatum*. The red oil stains your fingers when you pick the plant, and it is used externally to treat burns, neuralgia and inflammation. Some writers have associated this oil with the blood from St. John's beheading. An attractive pink infused oil can be made for external use. The plant thrives in the sunshine and springs up where trees have been felled.

Traditionally St. John's Wort was considered to be magically protective and a remedy for melancholy. It is now becoming well-known for its anti-depressant action. It is a nerve tonic which helps both nervous exhaustion and damage to nerves caused by diseases such as shingles and herpes.

PARTS USED The flowering tops.

DOSE 1 tsp dried/2 tsp fresh to a cup of boiling water, three times a day.

The flowers of St. John's Wort need to be harvested as soon as they begin to open.

CAUTION
This remedy is best avoided when you are spending time in bright sunlight.

DAMIANA

TURNERA DIFFUSA

Damiana grows in South America and the West Indies. It was previously called *Turnera aphrodisiaca* and is a tonic to the nervous system and the reproductive system. It raises the spirits and is particularly useful if sexual function is impaired. It is traditionally a remedy for men, but the stimulant and tonic effects work well for women too.

PARTS USED Leaves and stem.

DOSE 1 tsp to a cup of boiling water twice a day.

Damiana is harvested when flowering and dried for use as an anti-depressant, to relieve anxiety and to improve sexual function.

WILD OATS

AVENA SATIVA

Oats are an excellent tonic to the nervous system, giving both nourishment and energy. Anybody who has seen the effects of Oats on horses will understand their action. They are slightly stimulating and a long-term remedy for nervous exhaustion, lifting the mood while improving adaptability. Oats are also useful when there is disease of the nervous system such as shingles or herpes. A traditional breakfast of porridge is certainly a good idea. Oats contain vitamin E, iron, zinc, manganese and protein and are a good source of fibre, which helps to lower cholesterol levels.

PARTS USED Seeds and stalks.

DOSE There are many ways to take oats – in gruel, porridge, flapjacks, oatcakes and other dishes, as well as tea.

CAUTION
Oats are not suitable for those with a gluten sensitivity.

Oats are a good general tonic.

VERVAIN

VERBENA OFFICINALIS, HERB OF GRACE

An unassuming plant with tiny bluish-purple flowers which appears, like a mist, on waste ground and road-sides. Vervain has a long-documented reputation in the treatment of many physical and psychological problems. As a protective and purifying herb it was considered one of the most magical by both the Druids and the Romans – it has continued to be referred to in medical texts long after magic and medicine were separated.

Vervain is a nervous tonic with a slightly sedative action. It is useful for treating nervous exhaustion and symptoms of tension which include headaches, nausea and migraine. It has a bitter taste and has been used for gall bladder problems. It is also recommended for depression and combines well with Oats.

PARTS USED Leaves and flowers.

DOSE 1 tsp dried/2 tsp fresh to a cup of boiling water.

Lift your boughs of Vervain blue
Dipt in cold September dew
And dash the moisture chaste and clear,
O'er the ground and through the air.
Now the place is purged and pure.
WILLIAM MASON (1724–97)

CRAMP BARK

VIBURNUM OPULUS, GUELDER ROSE

A decorative wild bush which produces glorious white and pale pink spring flowers, followed by red berries among its crimson foliage in autumn. Gardeners know it as the snowball bush. Geoffrey Grigson in *The Englishman's Flora* (1958) said it had a smell like crisply fried, well-peppered trout! The fruits have been used in preserves and as a substitute for cranberries, and a spirit has been distilled from them. They are very tart, but are good mixed with Elder, Rowan and Blackberries in hedgerow jam.

Therapeutically, the use of Cramp Bark is a good illustration of the connection between body and mind. It reduces spasm whatever the cause and is therefore helpful for constipation, period pains, high blood pressure and feeling "uptight".

PARTS USED Dried bark.

DOSE 1 tsp to a cup of boiling water.

Viburnum opulus is a common hedgerow plant.

101

LAVENDER

The Lavender plant is always a delight.

LAVANDULA SPP.

Everybody knows this fragrant plant. Herbalists call it a thymoleptic, which means it raises the spirits. This, combined with its anti-infective action and relaxing properties, makes Lavender a powerful remedy. The essential oil is used externally for relaxation and to heal sores and burns. It is less well-known that Lavender can be taken internally in a tea or tincture. It reduces wind; indeed, Lavender was at one time used as a condiment. The flowers can be used to flavour biscuits, vinegar, puddings and ice creams. Lavender is an ideal remedy for irritation, indigestion and potential migraines. A few fresh or dried flowers added to teas made with other herbs, such as Nettle, will have a cheering effect.

PARTS USED Flowers and stalks.

DOSE ½ tsp to a cup of boiling water 3 times a day. Use infused oil for massage or in the bath.

Harvesting commercially grown Lavender.

ROSEMARY

ROSMARINUS OFFICINALIS

A familiar plant containing several active, aromatic oils. This sturdy shrub is often found in gardens. Like Lavender, it can be used both externally, in the form of essential or infused oil, and internally as a flavouring, tea or tincture.

The actions of Rosemary are centred on the head and womb. It increases the supply of blood to both. In the head it is helpful for cold headaches, forgetfulness (it symbolizes remembrance) and even premature baldness. In the womb and the gut it eases spasm due to poor circulation. With a general relaxing and anti-depressive action this is a remedy appropriate for many problems associated with poor circulation.

Externally, the oil can be used as an anti-microbial remedy and to reduce pain as well as to clear the head.

PARTS USED Leaves and flowers.

DOSE 1 tsp to a cup of boiling water 3 times a day.

Use Rosemary-infused oil for massage or in the bath.

The latin name for Rosemary, *Rosmarinus officinalis* means "dew of the sea".

MOTHERWORT

Motherwort requires moist soil and good drainage.

LEONURUS CARDIACA

This stately plant, with its strong, wine-coloured square stem, bears delicate mauve flowers within prickly, toothed calyces. Its name is thought to refer to the leaves being the shape of a lion's tail and *cardiaca* implies that this herb will strengthen the heart. In Britain it used to be grown for use as a remedy, while in the rest of Europe it is found wild. Motherwort makes a fine syrup and a refreshing, bitter tea.

It is a great calmer, especially if tension is causing palpitations or sweats. It improves and tones the circulatory system and is useful for relieving menstrual and menopausal problems. Motherwort can help to lower blood pressure and improve cardiac output during exercise.

According to Culpeper, it makes mothers joyful. It combines well with Lady's Mantle.

PARTS USED Leaves and flowers.

DOSE 1 tsp dried/2 tsp fresh to a cup of boiling water 3 times a day, or 2 tsp syrup.

CAUTION
Avoid in the first trimester of pregnancy.

Motherwort has always been associated with the sun.

CHASTE TREE

VITEX AGNUS-CASTUS, MONK'S PEPPER

The berries from this aromatic wayside bush found in southern Europe have a tradition of use by both women and men. Its common name reflects a slight anti-oestrogen effect which can cool passion: perhaps this property may account for its other common name – Monk's Pepper.

Many menstrual problems are a result of an excess of oestrogen, possibly due to use of the contraceptive pill or environmental pollution. Small doses of Chaste Tree can re-balance the hormones and reduce some of the symptoms of PMS, menopausal change, infertility, post-natal depression and irregular periods. It also increases milk production after birth. Altogether it is a soothing and much appreciated plant.

PARTS USED Dried ripe fruits.

DOSE 10–20 drops of tincture taken first thing in the morning.

Chaste Tree is a traditional symbol of virtue in southern Europe.

LADY'S MANTLE

ALCHEMILLA XANTHOCHLORA syn.
A. VULGARIS, VIRGIN'S CAPE

The unusual leaves of this plant resemble a cloak – hence its common names. Each leaf collects a shining drop of dew overnight. The name *Alchemilla* derives from the Arabic word for alchemy, a reference to its power to make a change. A larger species, *Alchemilla mollis*, is often grown as a foliage plant in gardens – it is thought to have similar properties.

As its name suggests, Lady's Mantle is a women's herb; like Chaste Tree, it helps to balance menstrual cycles. As a douche or wash, an infusion soothes itching and inflammation. A warming, drying remedy, it is useful for excessive bleeding and diarrhoea.

PARTS USED Leaves and flowers.

DOSE 1 tsp dried/2 tsp fresh to a cup of boiling water 3 times a day.

Alchemilla mollis.

EVENING PRIMROSE

OENOTHERA BIENNIS

A beautiful plant, luminous in the twilight, Evening Primrose is generous in its actions and appearance. A statuesque plant growing over 1 m/3 ft tall, its large pale yellow flowers open in the early evening and quickly fade to be replaced by tubular seed pods. It produces many seeds and spreads freely.

The whole plant is edible, and the oil from the seeds is a source of essential fatty acids and therefore useful as a nutritional supplement. It is also used externally for eczema and other dry skin conditions. Taken internally, Evening Primrose oil reduces cholesterol levels and benefits the circulation generally. Supplements are recommended for sufferers from rheumatoid arthritis, multiple sclerosis and diabetes. Evening Primrose oil can also be helpful for PMS and other inflammatory conditions.

PARTS USED Oil produced from seeds.

DOSE Capsules as directed.

CAUTION
Avoid in cases of epilepsy.

Above: The Evening Primrose likes to grow in dry, sunny conditions. Although the flower of *Oenothera* each last only a short time, they are produced in long succession.

Right: Evening Primrose capsules are easily available commercially.

LIME BLOSSOM

TILIA x *EUROPAEA*, LINDEN BLOSSOM

Found, according to Culpeper, "in parks and gentlemen's gardens", the tall upstanding Lime tree with its warm, honey-scented blossom is a great favourite. Lime blossom honey is prized and the infusion *tilleul* is popular in France. Grigson warned that you should pick your own flowers because those harvested and dried commercially taste of newspaper!

The pale, soft wood of Lime trees is used for delicate carving and produces artist's charcoal. The fibres are used in basketry and rope-making.

Lime is no less useful medicinally, being relaxing and cleansing. It makes a helpful tea for fevers and flu especially if combined with Yarrow and Peppermint. It encourages sweating and thus helps the body through fevers. It is also used to reduce hardening of the arteries and high blood pressure. It can relieve vascular headaches, including migraine.

Lime Blossom combines well with Lemon Balm to ease nervous tension.

PARTS USED Flowers, including the pale yellowish bracts.

DOSE 1 tsp dried/2 tsp fresh to a cup of boiling water 3 times a day.

The deliciously scented flowers of the Lime tree should be collected when they have just opened.

Lime Blossom tea.

Dried Lime Blossom.

MINT

Peppermint has to be propagated by root division in the spring. It is an invasive plant and needs cutting back regularly.

MENTHA SPP.

Peppermint (*Mentha piperita*) is the most used of the mint family, and is a hybrid between Spearmint and Watermint, but most mints have some therapeutic effect. The plants are robust and spread enthusiastically, although they need plenty of moisture to grow well. Peppermint seems always to have been popular; there is evidence that it was cultivated by the Egyptians and certainly the Greeks and Romans used it. Roman women ate it after drinking wine to mask the breath.

Mint is used as flavouring and medicine, chiefly because of the action of volatile oils. This is a cheering plant which reduces spasm in the gut and increases the production of digestive secretions. It's easy to see why after-dinner mints are so popular. Mint is also used in drinks, jellies and sauces.

Peppermint is antiseptic and anti-parasitic, and will reduce itching. It has a temporary anaesthetic effect on the skin and gives the impression of cooling. It is included in lotions for massaging aching muscles, and makes an effective footbath for tired, hot feet.

It is included in traditional teas for alleviating the symptoms of colds and flu.

PARTS USED Leaves and flowers.

DOSE 1 tsp dried/2 tsp fresh to a cup of boiling water.

CAUTION
Excessive use of mint can damage the gut or cause headaches. Avoid it if you have a peptic ulcer.

PASQUE FLOWER

ANEMONE PULSATILLA, WIND FLOWER
This is perhaps one of the most beautiful medicinal herbs. The vivid purple flowers appear among greyish foliage in the spring and are therefore named for Easter (from the Middle English word *Pasch*).

Pasque Flower is a sedative, bactericidal, anti-spasmodic painkiller, with a particular affinity with the reproductive organs. Thus it is used for all types of pain affecting male and female genital organs, with or without an element of tension or agitation.
PARTS USED Dried leaves and flowers.
DOSE A very low dose is needed – it is advisable to consult a herbalist or buy a commercial preparation.

CAUTION
Do not use the fresh plant.

The delicate Pasque Flower is now a rarity in the wild.

MARJORAM

ORIGANUM VULGARE
There are many species of Marjoram, whose botanical name comes from the Greek and means "joy of the mountain". Sweet Marjoram (*Origanum majorana*) is commonly used in potpourri, and as a culinary herb it is popular in Greek and Italian cooking. Wild Marjoram, usually referred to as Oregano when used in cooking, has a spicy fragrance, small, rounded leaves and tiny pink flowers.

Medicinally, Marjoram reduces depression and is helpful for nervous headaches. It contains volatile oils which are antispasmodic so it is useful in soothing digestive upsets.

The infused oil can be used in the bath to relieve stiffness or rubbed on to soothe sore and aching joints or muscles.
PARTS USED Leaves.
DOSE 1 tsp dried/2 tsp fresh to a cup of boiling water, twice a day.

The oil distilled from Marjoram is used commercially in toiletries and perfumes.

Herbal Recipes

You can't always avoid stress, but there are plenty of things that you can do to help yourself cope better when life presents a challenge.

Diet really does make a difference. Make sure that you eat proper, healthy meals with lots of vitamin-rich fruit and vegetables and no artificial additives (add herbs instead, to contribute flavour to your food, as well as extra goodness).

Try to reduce stimulants such as tea, coffee, alcohol and cola – drink plenty of water or herb tea. Exercise is important too: it dispels excess adrenaline and improves relaxation and sleep.

Stressful events are likely to disrupt your appetite and your ability to rest, but both are vital to enable you to cope well. Use herbal remedies as your allies to improve your digestion, help you to relax and improve your adaptability.

The recipes that follow are designed to help

Peppermint is cooling and counteracts tiredness. The essential oil is ideal for using in a refreshing footbath.

you through some of the difficult times that assail everyone from time to time. As long as you don't exceed the doses stated, and as long as you are sure that you are using the right plant, it is safe to experiment with these suggestions to find the best remedy for you. But remember to seek professional help if a problem persists.

Facing page: Handling herbs and preparing herbal teas and other recipes can be a relaxing experience.

Herbs in many forms: Lavender as an infused oil, Lime Blossom as a tincture and fresh Rosemary stems.

PREPARING FOR A BIG DAY

If you are getting ready for an important event in your life you are bound to want to be sure that you will cope well. If you are revising for exams or some other important test you'll need to be able to concentrate when you are working, but also be able to switch off and rest when you stop.

As well as paying special attention to your diet, you might take a multivitamin supplement or yeast tablets to nourish your nervous system with plenty of vitamin B. Try to take regular exercise, and release the build-up of tension with a relaxing massage or even just a herbal bath. However busy you are, try to do something for pleasure each day.

Use meditation to calm the mind and help you wind down.

SUSTAINING TEA
Boil 1 tsp each dried Licorice and Ginseng root in 600 ml/1 pint/ 2½ cups water for 10 minutes. Pour the decoction over 3 tsp dried Borage. Allow to steep for

10 minutes. Strain.

Drink one cupful, hot or cold, three times a day.

OTHER SUGGESTIONS
• Make Borage tea and sweeten to taste with a solid bar of Licorice.
• Buy Ginseng capsules and take as directed for three weeks before the big event.
• Eat a big bowl of porridge for breakfast every morning.
• Treat yourself to a flapjack.

CAUTION
Licorice is not recommended for those with high blood pressure.

Borage improves the production of adrenaline in times of stress.

HERBAL REMEDIES THAT WILL HELP
• Ginseng (*Panax* for men and *Eleutherococcus* for women).
• Wild Oats
• Licorice
• Borage

Ginseng helps concentration and improves clarity of mind.

COPING WITH A DIFFICULT TIME

However well you normally manage, sometimes life just gets hard. Maybe there's a new baby in the family, a relative is ill and depending on you, you're moving house or very busy at work. It's important to remember to look after yourself when extra demands are made on you. Diet, sleep and exercise are all crucial, and herbs can help during stressful times.

HERBAL REMEDIES THAT WILL HELP
- Wild Oats
- Licorice
- Borage
- Skullcap, Wood Betony or Vervain, according to your usual reaction to stress.

DE-STRESSING TEA
Put 1 tsp of each of the dried herbs listed above into a jug, tea pot or cafetière. Top up with boiling water and leave to infuse for 10 minutes. Strain and sweeten with more Licorice (avoid if you have high blood pressure). Drink one cup, warm, three times a day.

Rub a little Lavender oil on the temples and forehead when you are under pressure to help you relax.

Skullcap calms anxiety.

Right: Licorice supports the adrenal glands.

RELIEVING PMT

Women experience a variety of symptoms before their period. Sometimes it can be good to acknowledge that you are cyclic and changeable and need, if you can, to do different things at different times in the month. Unfortunately, this isn't always possible. If you feel too much "not yourself" at this time, it may help you to eat particularly vitamin- and mineral-rich foods. For the second half of your cycle eat plenty of fruit and salad, especially bananas, carrots, nuts and grapes. Cut right down on salt and processed food and eat little and often to avoid cravings.

Eating delicious fruits is a pleasurable way to ease the effects of PMT.

> ### HERBAL REMEDIES THAT WILL HELP
> - Chaste Tree
> - Evening Primrose
> - Vervain
> - Lady's Mantle

A LONG-TERM SOLUTION
Take Chaste Tree tincture, 12 drops every morning for three months. Take Evening Primrose oil capsules as directed on the packet.

VERVAIN AND LADY'S MANTLE TEA
Put 1 tsp each dried Vervain and dried Lady's Mantle into a pot. Add 300 ml/½ pint/1¼ cups boiling water. Steep for 10 minutes. Strain and sweeten to taste.

Take one cup twice a day from day 14 of your cycle, or two weeks after your period starts.

Capsules of Evening Primrose oil provide essential fatty acids, often lacking with PMT.

EASING PERIOD PAIN

Pain during or just before periods is due to contraction in the muscles of the womb which reduces blood flow causing the muscles to ache. Exercise and heat will increase the circulation of blood.

Cramp Bark, as its name implies, reduces spasm, and Rosemary is a circulatory stimulant, which is particularly associated with the womb and the head. Its aromatic oils are cheering and relaxing. A decoction of Ginger drunk frequently before and during your period is helpful too.

A hot water bottle can be comforting, but for added benefit try using a hot, aromatic compress.

HERBAL REMEDIES THAT WILL HELP
- Cramp Bark
- Rosemary
- Ginger

Ginger and Rosemary.

CRAMP BARK AND ROSEMARY COMPRESS

1 Boil 2 tsp Cramp Bark in 600 ml/1 pint/2½ cups water for 10–15 minutes. Add 2 tsp dried Rosemary. Leave to steep for 15 minutes, then strain.

2 Soak a clean cotton cloth or bandage in the liquid. When cool enough to handle, wring out the cloth.

3 Place the hot compress on your abdomen and relax.

HELPING WITH THE MENOPAUSE

The menopause doesn't have to be a problem, but the changes in women's lives and bodies can cause difficulties. Think of these years as a time to look after yourself and rethink old habits.

HERBAL REMEDIES THAT WILL HELP
- Chaste Tree
- Motherwort
- Sage
- Lime Blossom
- Licorice

WHEN YOUR PERIODS FIRST BECOME IRREGULAR
Take 10 drops of Chaste Tree tincture each morning for three months.

REDUCING NIGHT SWEATS
Dissolve 1 tsp honey in a cup of hot water. Add 2 drops of Sage essential oil.

Drink the mixture before you go to bed, then cover yourself with a dry towel and rest. Add any remaining tea to your bath water the following day.

ALLEVIATING HOT SWEATS

1 Put 1 tsp each dried Motherwort and Sage in a cup. Pour on 600 ml/1 pint/2½ cups boiling water. Sweeten with Licorice (omit this if you have high blood pressure).

2 Allow to cool, then sip throughout the day.

CAUTION
Do not drink Sage tea continually. Take for three weeks, then avoid for at least one week.

Sage is a tonic that helps to see the way through changes.

Motherwort helps to strengthen the heart.

RELAXING TENSE MUSCLES

Muscles can become tense as a result of anxiety; this often causes slightly raised shoulders or contracted back muscles. The effort of maintaining your muscles in this semi-contracted state is tiring and may eventually result in perpetual spasm and bad postural habits. Your neck will feel stiff and your back may ache. Tight neck muscles can also prevent adequate blood flow to your head and cause tension headaches.

Another cause of muscle tension is spending a long time in the same position. This can occur if you are bending your head to look at a computer screen or driving a long distance. It's important to move frequently to release the muscles. Rotate your head or stand up and stretch, and remember to take regular breaks from

HERBAL REMEDIES THAT WILL HELP
- Lavender
- Marjoram
- Rosemary
- Cramp Bark

Tension can build up in the neck and shoulders causing stiffness.

working or driving. Massaging the neck and shoulders with a relaxing oil can help.

COLD INFUSED OIL OF LAVENDER
Fill a jar with lavender heads and cover with clear vegetable oil. Allow to steep on a windowsill for a month, shaking the jar every day. Strain and bottle.

Massage into a stiff neck or back. This oil can also be added to the bath to keep your skin soft and perfumed while encouraging

relaxation. Similar oils can be made from Marjoram (which is anti-spasmodic) or Rosemary.

Dilute concentrated essential oil before use on the skin. Add 2 drops of oil to 4 tsp of grapeseed or almond oil.

Home-made infused oils are cheap to make and very effective.

CALMING ANXIETY

We all know what it feels like to be excited – just remember waiting for a party when you were a child. This is a great part of life, but inappropriate or excessive excitement, often combined with frustration, will lead to anxiety. Think of a commuter pacing up and down the station platform, late for a meeting, or a parent tossing and turning in bed when their teenage child is still out late at night. In situations like these you are producing too much adrenaline. Your body is primed for "fight or flight" with nowhere to go: your heart is racing, your muscles are tense and your chest is expanded. All these conditions are appropriate before a race, but not in bed or on the train.

Anxiety can cause many symptoms, including palpitations, sweating, irritability and sleeplessness. Herbs can help very effectively with all of these.

Rescue Remedy, a Bach Flower Remedy which is readily available over the counter, can be used if you feel frightened or anxious – just put two drops on your tongue.

HERBAL REMEDIES
THAT WILL HELP
- *To help your nervous system adapt:*
  - Wild Oats
  - Vervain
  - St. John's Wort
  - Skullcap
  - Wood Betony

These are all nervous tonics. Choose whichever one suits you best and combine it with a specific remedy for the symptom that troubles you most.
- *To ease palpitations:* Motherwort or Passionflower.
- *To reduce sweating:* Valerian or Motherwort.
- *To help you sleep:* Passionflower or Valerian.

Two drops of Rescue Remedy on the tongue can help prevent a panic attack.

Motherwort relieves palpitations.

LONG-TERM TREATMENT FOR ANXIETY

Put 1 tsp of each of your three chosen dried herbs into a pot (use only ½ tsp Passionflower). Add 600 ml/1 pint/2½ cups boiling water and leave to steep for 10–15 minutes. Strain.

Sit down and drink one cup three times a day. Do this for at least two to four weeks.

Above: Oats are a food for both the body and the mind.

Above: A soothing herbal tea will help to reduce over-reaction.

Right: Lavender and Hops both reduce tension and encourage relaxing sleep.

RELIEVING COUGHS AND COLDS

A cough is a natural reflex reaction to any irritation, inflammation or blockage in the airways. It often accompanies an infection such as a cold or bronchitis. By keeping the bronchial tubes open and clear, coughing can be of vital importance, and treatment should be aimed at making the cough more effective rather than just suppressing it.

WARMING GINGER AND LEMON TEA
Ginger is stimulating and encourages sweating to eliminate toxins and dispel catarrh. Make a decoction using 115 g/4 oz fresh Ginger root, the rind of 1 lemon and a pinch of cayenne in 600 ml/1 pint/ 2 ½ cups water. Simmer for 20 minutes, then add the juice of the lemon and sip a small cupful at a time, sweetened to taste with honey.

HERBAL REMEDIES THAT WILL HELP
- Borage
- Lavender
- Sage
- Hyssop
- Coltsfoot
- Marshmallow
- Thyme
- Licorice

▲ A decoction of Ginger and lemon relieves the discomfort of a cold.

TO SOOTHE A DRY COUGH
Put 15 g/½ oz dried Borage flowers and leaves with 15 g/½ oz dried Thyme into a pan with two 5 cm/2 in cinnamon sticks and 600 ml/1 pint/2 ½ cups water. Simmer for 20 minutes then strain off the herbs. Simmer the liquid, uncovered, until reduced by half. Add the juice of 1 small lemon and 115 g/4 oz/½ cup honey and simmer gently for a further 5 minutes. Bottle and store in a cool place, taking 5 ml/1 tsp, as required.

▶ Vitamin C-rich lemons with fresh ginger.

SOOTHING A SORE THROAT

Sore throats are more and more common nowadays, with increased airborne pollution and smoky, dry atmospheres in air-conditioned buildings. The irritation can range from an annoying tickle to a rasping soreness, and may be linked to other infections. Gargling with an infusion of herbs or sipping herbal teas can ease the discomfort.

HERBAL GARGLE

Put 15 ml/1 tbsp each dried Sage and Thyme in a jug and add 600 ml/1 pint/2 ½ cups boiling water. Cover and leave for 30 minutes, then strain off the herbs and stir in 30 ml/2 tbsp cider vinegar, 10 ml/2 tsp honey and 5 ml/1 tsp cayenne pepper. Use as a gargle at the first sign of a sore throat. It can also be taken internally, 10 ml/2 tsp at a time, 2–3 times a day. Hyssop and Horehound can be used in the same way to make a strong gargle.

HERBAL REMEDIES THAT WILL HELP
- Sage
- Thyme
- Licorice
- Hyssop
- Horehound

▲ Fresh Thyme and Sage are the raw ingredients for an antiseptic gargle to ease a sore throat.

◀ Horehound (with silvery leaves) combines well with aromatic Hyssop (with blue flowers) for a gargle to combat a cough.

RECOVERING FROM NERVOUS EXHAUSTION

You are much more likely to get ill or depressed after or during a long period of hard work or heavy emotional demands. This can easily happen to teachers at the end of term, or to those who care for disabled or sick relations on a long-term basis. Herbal remedies will give your nervous system some support at times like this.

HERBAL REMEDIES THAT WILL HELP
- Wild Oats
- Licorice
- St. John's Wort
- Skullcap
- Borage
- Wood Betony

Try to find ways to reduce the impact of everyday stress.

REVITALIZING TEA
Mix equal portions of all the dried herbs listed. Put 3–4 tsp of the mixture into a pot with a lid. Add 600 ml/1 pint/2½ cups boiling water. Allow to steep for 10 minutes. Strain.

Drink three or four cups of this tea a day.

The delicate, star-shaped flowers of Borage help to raise the spirits.

Make a herbal tea from a blend of supportive herbs when you are feeling exhausted.

Wood Betony.

TONICS FOR CONVALESCENCE

It is easy to forget that, even if your symptoms have gone, your body needs time to recover after an illness. Dealing with disease depletes your immune system and, if you do not give yourself time to recoup, you will become more vulnerable to post-viral syndrome or recurrent infections. The old-fashioned concept of a tonic is useful. Wild Oats and St. John's Wort support the nervous system, Vervain promotes relaxation and digestion and Licorice and Borage restore the adrenal glands.

Vitamin C supplements should be continued for several weeks after an illness – take at least 1-2 grams each day. Plenty of rest is important, as is a nourishing diet. Alfalfa sprouts are a rich source of vitamins and minerals.

TONIC TEA

Put ½ tsp of each of the listed dried herbs into a small pot. Add boiling water. Flavour with Peppermint or Licorice to taste.

(Avoid Licorice if you suffer from high blood pressure.) Allow to steep for 10 minutes. Strain. Drink three or four cups, warm, each day for at least three weeks.

Drinking a tonic tea every day will encourage recovery.

Citrus fruits are a well-known source of vitamin C.

Borage restores the adrenal glands.

HERBAL REMEDIES THAT WILL HELP
- Wild Oats
- Vervain
- St. John's Wort
- Borage
- Licorice

123

RELIEVING WINTER BLUES

Try some of the many different herb teas to find one you enjoy.

HERBAL REMEDIES THAT WILL HELP
- St. John's Wort
- Wild Oats
- Ginseng
- Rosemary

The old herbalists thought that the appearance of a plant held a clue to its healing action. For instance, Pilewort (Lesser Celandine) has roots which resemble haemorrhoids, and it does indeed make an effective ointment for piles. The flowers of St. John's Wort resemble nothing so much as the sun. The plant thrives in sunlight and is known to have anti-depressant effects. There is no better herb than this to take if you are depressed in the winter, when sunlight is in short supply.

Wild Oats also help by strengthening the nervous system and keeping you warm. Rosemary, an evergreen plant, will improve circulation to the head and keep the mind clear.

Ginseng capsules can be taken for a month in the early autumn to help you adapt to the transition between seasons.

WINTER BRIGHTENER
Combine 2 tsp dried St. John's Wort with 1 tsp dried Rosemary. Add 250 ml/8 fl oz/1 cup boiling water. Allow to steep for 10 minutes. Strain.

Drink three times a day throughout the winter.

St. John's Wort thrives in sunlight.

Rosemary helps to clear the mind.

LIFTING DEPRESSION

Depression illustrates well the connection between body and mind: physical and emotional energy are both depleted when you are in a depressed state. Both will benefit from a healthy diet with plenty of raw, vital foods, nuts, seeds and B vitamins. A multivitamin and mineral supplement may be useful until you feel energetic enough to prepare good food. Try also to cut down on stimulants, such as caffeine, which tend to exhaust both body and mind.

The restorative tea suggested will restore the health of your nervous system while having a slightly stimulating effect.

There are many tasty ways to include the goodness of Oats in your diet.

St. John's Wort is a nerve tonic.

HERBAL REMEDIES THAT WILL HELP
- St. John's Wort
- Wild Oats
- Damiana

RESTORATIVE TEA
Mix equal parts of each of the dried herbs listed. Put 2 tsp of the mixture into a pot. Add 600 ml/ 1 pint/2½ cups boiling water. Allow to steep for 10 minutes and then strain.

Drink one cup of this tea three times a day.

DIGESTIVES

Many people suffer from digestive upsets when they are stressed. This is because the "fight or flight" activity of the sympathetic nervous system tends to suppress digestive processes. The result may be indigestion, loss of appetite, wind, diarrhoea or irritable bowel.

The recipes below will relax the nervous system, encouraging parasympathetic activity and reducing spasm in the gut.

HERBAL REMEDIES THAT WILL HELP
- Chamomile
- Lemon Balm
- Peppermint
- Licorice
- Cramp Bark
- Hops
- Fennel, Caraway, Dill, Cumin

TO CALM BUTTERFLIES, OR A NERVOUS STOMACH
Chamomile, Hops and Lemon Balm can be combined in a tea, or select the best combination for

you. Lemon Balm and Chamomile can be taken as frequently as you find suitable.

Put 1 tsp each Lemon Balm, dried Chamomile flowers and Peppermint into a small tea pot or cafetière. Fill with boiling water and allow to steep for at least 10 minutes. Strain and drink at least three times a day or after meals. Hops can be added to settle the stomach in the evening.

Fresh Lemon Balm makes a delicious tea and calms the stomach.

CAUTION
Hops are sedative, so should only be added at night. Avoid Hops if you are depressed or lacking in sexual energy. Avoid Licorice if you have high blood pressure.

Chamomile tea makes an ideal after-dinner drink.

Lemon Balm acts as a digestive.

TO RELIEVE WIND AND COLIC

In a small saucepan, boil 1 tsp each Fennel seeds and Cramp Bark with about 300 ml/½ pint/1¼ cups water. Add 1 tsp dried Peppermint. Allow to steep for 10 minutes. Strain and drink.

TO EASE CONSTIPATION

Make a decoction of Cramp Bark and Fennel as above, but add 1 tsp Licorice root.

If constipation is a recurrent condition, 1 tsp Linseeds added daily to your breakfast cereal can be helpful.

HANGOVER REMEDIES

Most people know what a hangover feels like – a combination of headache, nausea, fuzzy head and depression. Most of these symptoms are connected with the liver being overloaded and unable to perform its many crucial functions properly. Bitter herbs stimulate the liver and hurry along its detoxification work. Vervain is bitter and Lavender aids digestion; both herbs lift the spirits.

If you have a hangover it is also advisable to drink plenty of water and take extra vitamin C.

HERBAL REMEDIES THAT WILL HELP
- Vervain
- Lavender

The lavender plant even looks calming.

MORNING-AFTER TEA
Put 1 tsp dried Vervain and ½ tsp Lavender flowers into a pot. Add 600 ml/1 pint/2½ cups boiling water and cover to keep in the volatile oils. Allow to steep for 10 minutes. Strain and sweeten with a little honey.

Sip this tea as often as you like throughout the day until you start to feel better.

Left: Add honey to sweeten any tea or decoction.

Blackcurrants and citrus fruits are especially rich in vitamin C.

RELIEVING HEADACHES

Headaches are a common symptom of stress. Often they are caused by tension in the neck and upper back muscles. This can prevent adequate blood supply to the head and thus lead to pain. Both massage and exercise can be a great help in easing this kind of headache.

HERBAL REMEDIES THAT WILL HELP
- Lavender
- Rosemary
- Wood Betony

LAVENDER OR ROSEMARY SCENTED BATH

Pour a few drops of essential oil or some infused oil into a hot bath. Lie back and relax! Even better, tie a bunch of the fresh herb under the hot tap as you fill the bath (this avoids oily smears around the bath).

Two drops of essential oil of Lavender can be mixed with 1 tsp hot or cold water and rubbed directly on to the head during times of stress.

Lavender or Rosemary oil can be rubbed into the temples.

Hang a muslin bag of fresh or dried herbs under the hot tap.

SOOTHING TEA

Put 1 tsp dried Wood Betony and ½ tsp dried Lavender or Rosemary into a cup. Top up with boiling water and leave to steep for 10 minutes.

Strain and drink. Repeat hourly throughout the day.

Make time to relax completely in a hot, scented bath.

Rosemary.

129

REVITALIZING THE LIBIDO

Sometimes depression or anxiety makes happy sexual functioning difficult. This may be because your energy is too low, or it may be connected with a hormone imbalance. Damiana stimulates both the nervous and hormonal systems. It has constituents which convert in the body to hormones. Vervain releases tension and stress and was traditionally used as an aphrodisiac. Wild Oats and Ginger root are both stimulating too.

HERBAL REMEDIES THAT WILL HELP
- Damiana
- Vervain
- Wild Oats
- Ginger

Teas or decoctions made with the right herbs can help restore energy of all kinds, including sexual energy.

Ginger fires the blood.

ENERGIZING TEA
Put 1 tsp dried Damiana and 1 tsp dried Vervain into a pot. Add 600 ml/1 pint/2½ cups of boiling water. Leave to steep for 10 minutes.

Strain and flavour with Licorice, Ginger or honey. Drink two cups a day.

Dried herb tea.

130

ENHANCING SLEEP

There are many types of insomnia and many types of people. If you can't sleep it is best to experiment with the remedies below to find the one herb or combination of herbs which suits you. If you haven't been sleeping well for a long period, include a nervous system tonic to improve the long-term situation.

Drink teas made from relaxing herbs in the evenings. Lavender oil in a hot bath before bed and on the pillow will help. You could try a Hop pillow too.

Remember to allow time at the end of the day to relax and wind down. Exercise, meditation and yoga all help with sleep difficulties.

SLEEPY TEA
Put 1 tsp each dried Chamomile, Vervain and Lemon Balm into a pot. Add about 600 ml/1 pint/2½ cups boiling water. Leave to steep for 10 minutes.

Strain and drink one cup after supper. Warm the rest and drink before going to bed.

If you continue to have problems sleeping, add a decoction of 1 tsp Valerian root or ½ tsp dried Hops or Californian Poppy to the herb blend.

Chamomile tea.

Lemon Balm.

HERBAL REMEDIES THAT WILL HELP
- Lemon Balm
- Chamomile
- Valerian
- Californian Poppy
- Vervain
- Passionflower (use only ½ tsp a day)
- Hops (use only ½ tsp a day)

You can make or buy a herb pillow to encourage sound sleep.

HEALTH AND HARMONY: *Natural Well-being*

WE HAVE BECOME accustomed to thinking of medicine as a crisis treatment for when we are sick, but one of the strengths of natural therapies is their value in countering the effects of stress and actually helping prevent illness. By taking some simple and pleasurable steps to restore and enhance our own vital energy and inner harmony, we can actively reduce the impact of the worries and stresses that we encounter in our daily lives.

STRATEGIES FOR COPING WITH STRESS

You can improve your general health and well-being, and thus your defences against illness,
by understanding what causes you stress and by learning how to avoid it or adapt to it.

Above: Many people find the help of a trained counsellor of great benefit
during times of exceptional stress.

A BALANCED LIFESTYLE
There are basically two aspects
to stress reduction: lifestyle
modification and relaxation.
Modifying your lifestyle could
mean changing your job and
reassessing your goals in life, or
simply adopting a more open
attitude to what you are doing.
Gaining a sense of control over
events lessens their stressful impact.

A situation that is causing you
unbearable stress can be made
easier by asking for help and
support from family and friends:
talking to someone helps you to
see a problem more clearly.
Getting regular breaks from a
stressful lifestyle will help you to
cope better and avoid having a
situation reach a crisis point.

Left: However busy you are,
making time for yourself is
important in enabling you to
cope with stress.

SYMPTOMS OF STRESS

The symptoms of stress vary, but if you experience some or all of the following, you may be over-stressed:

• Constantly on edge, with a very short fuse and ready to explode for no real reason.
• Feeling on the verge of tears much of the time.
• Difficulty in concentrating, decision-making or with memory.
• Always tired even after a full night's sleep.
• Sleep itself is disturbed and unrefreshing.
• A feeling of not being able to cope, that it's all too much.
• Poor appetite, or else nibbling food without really being hungry.
• No sense of fun or enjoyment in life.
• Mistrustful of everybody, unable to enjoy company.

Above: Learning the flowing movements of Tai Chi will both relax your muscles and focus your mind.

Left: Meditation can be helpful in calming your mind and helping you through stressful events.

LEARNING TO RELAX

Daily relaxation represents the most important element of maintaining health and vitality. You might try a class in relaxation techniques, Yoga or Tai Chi, or have some professional massage treatments. Deep relaxation is not the same as sleep, and to gain full benefit from therapies such as meditation or massage, it is important not to fall asleep while relaxing. However, you will benefit more from a night's sleep, and awake feeling more refreshed, if you are mentally and physically relaxed before you go to bed.

EXERCISE

A certain amount of physical exercise is important, but take this in a way that you find pleasurable – it could be as simple as a brisk 20-minute walk in the fresh air every day. Exercise not only helps to use up excess adrenalin, but builds up physical and mental stamina. Deeper breathing will supply more oxygen to the brain, which is the first essential nourishment it needs. Daily exercise will help you to relax and sleep properly.

Above and left: Exercising can be fun as well as beneficial.

A HEALTHY DIET

One of the most obvious and successful ways in which we can affect our health is through nutrition. A healthy diet involves eating foods that provide all the nourishment that our bodies need for growth, tissue repair, energy to carry out vital internal processes and to stay fit and active. Try to eat a well-balanced diet rich in fibre, grains and vegetables; cut down on sugar and salt as well as coffee, tea, alcohol and carbonated soft drinks. Three key words are freshness, wholeness and variety. As far as possible make fresh foods the major part of your food intake – fresh fruit and vegetables, freshly cooked bread, pasta and other grains, and a little freshly prepared meat, poultry, fish or other protein-containing foods. Cut back on processed foods as much as you can. Above all, enjoy food: there is a lot of pleasure to be gained from the taste and aromas of a varied diet.

Above: Drink at least two litres of water a day to flush out toxins that build up in the body.

Left: A healthy diet need not be boring if you use variety and imagination in your food preparation.

RELAXING YOUR BODY

Most people tend to hold in patterns of tension arising from everyday cares and worries, bad posture and lack of exercise. These patterns make you feel stiff and unbending, and directly interfere with your movements. Inflexibility within the body can in turn affect mental flexibility, and you can become stuck in thought as well as in action.

EXERCISE

Regular exercise not only frees your body, but can also help you to think and act in a less restricted way. Choose forms of exercise that you enjoy and can easily incorporate into your daily routine: walking up and down stairs rather than taking the lift (elevator) is a simple example. Weekend walks, swimming, gardening, cycling or dancing can all help. You may find it helpful to join a class: with exercise like aerobics, low-impact exercises or weight-training, it is essential to make sure that you are doing the movements safely and correctly.

A short daily programme of stretching will strengthen muscles, ligaments and tendons, helping you to walk taller and more gracefully, and increasing your vigour and vitality. For centuries,

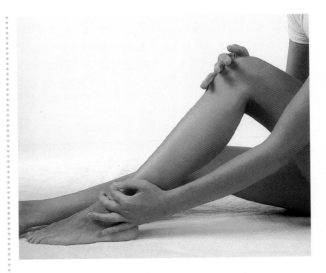

Above: Gentle strokes up the leg aid circulation.

stretching has formed an essential part of the physical exercises that are one aspect of Yoga, the ancient Indian system of self-improvement that embraces the body, mind and spirit. There are Yoga classes in almost every town, and the best way to learn is from a trained, supportive teacher.

Tai Chi is another ancient form of slow, graceful and rhythmic exercise. The movements gently tone and strengthen the organs and muscles, improve circulation and posture, and relax both mind and body. Again, it is important to find a class that you feel comfortable in.

THERAPEUTIC TOUCH

The use of touch to give comfort or to express love is as old as humankind, and is something humans share with animals as an instinctive way of bonding and sharing. Anyone who has experienced the physical tensions that accompany stressful situations will not be surprised to learn that massage is one of the most successful ways to relax those painful, knotted muscles. As a stress-reliever, it is probably without equal.

Massage can have a wonderful effect not only on our muscles but on our whole sense of well-being. Touch is one of the most crucial senses, and the need for human touch remains constant throughout life.

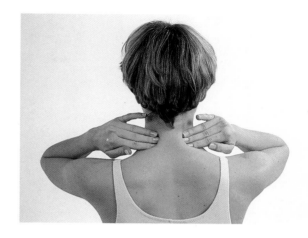

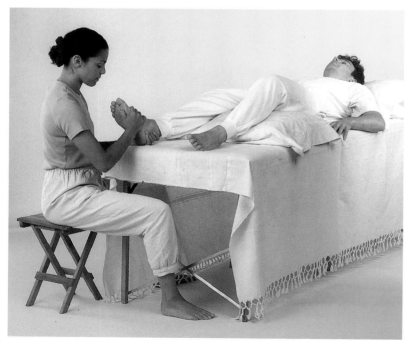

Above: Gentle neck massage provides effective relief for most tension headaches.

Left: Reflexology works to relax muscle tension. During treatment all areas of the feet are stimulated to relax muscles and increase circulation to all parts of the body. The immediate effect of this is to achieve a deep state of relaxation.

LOOSENING-UP EXERCISES

This sequence of loosening-up exercises will be enough on its own to get you more mobile, and will also be helpful to prepare you for more strenuous exercise. Try to breathe freely and comfortably when doing these and any other exercises, and remain aware of your body's response to the movements. If breathing becomes difficult or your heart races, stop, and ask your doctor's advice on suitable exercise.

SHOULDER AND NECK

1 To loosen the shoulders and ease neck tension, try slowly rolling your shoulders in a circle, lifting them right up as they move around, and then dropping them down again.

2 Stretch the neck muscles by slowly dropping your head to the side, towards one shoulder and then the other, repeating three or four times.

3 Then gently swing your head in an arc, from one side across your chest to the other side. Repeat the swing three or four times, keeping control of the movement all the time.

ARMS AND ABDOMEN

1 Swing your arms forwards in large circles to begin to loosen the shoulder joints, then reverse the action and swing them backwards to open up the chest.

2 Facing forwards, twist your arms from one side to the other, letting them move loosely.

3 Continue the movement, allowing your head and trunk to move sideways with the arm swings. Twist right round, keeping your head in line with your arms.

4 Bend sideways from the waist, keeping your hips still and moving your hand down towards your knee. Return to an upright position, then bend to the other side.

5 Extend this movement into a bigger stretch by raising one arm in the air and bending sideways. Repeat the movement in the opposite direction.

BENDING AND SQUATTING

1 With legs about shoulder-width apart, bend forwards as far as you can, keeping your legs straight.

2 Steadily return to the upright position. Repeat the action. If this is difficult, keep the legs slightly bent when bending forward, and gradually work on straightening the legs while leaning forwards.

3 With hands on your head or hips, squat down, keeping your back straight and heels off the ground.

4 Come back to a standing position, rising up on to your toes as you do so. Repeat the exercise several times.

5 Try jogging, running or jumping on the spot (in place).

CAUTION
If you suffer from any back or neck problems, you may be better off with a rebounder (small trampoline) or using a step to go up and down to reduce impact – get professional advice if you are unsure.

FLOOR EXERCISES

1 To tone and strengthen the abdominal muscles, try sitting on the floor, with knees bent and hands clasped around them. Lean back as far as is comfortable, using your arms to support your weight. Breathe out as you do so and hold for 5 seconds if possible.

2 Repeat at least five times. As your muscles improve, try placing your hands behind your head, so that the abdominal muscles do more work.

3 Get on to all fours on the floor, making sure that your hands are directly below your shoulders, and your knees are in line with your hips. Keep your back and neck in a straight line.

4 Then stretch and arch your back upwards, dropping your head down. Hold this position for a few seconds, then return to the first position. Repeat several times.

CAUTION
If you find you have any pain or discomfort when doing these exercises, get advice. If you find you prefer doing exercises with others, to music or even while singing along yourself, then do so and have fun!

SELF-MASSAGE

Aching, tense muscles are undoubtedly most usually experienced in the neck and shoulders. As you get tired, your posture tends to droop, and the rounded shape makes your neck and shoulders ache even more. Although it is most relaxing to lie down and have someone else massage away the tension, you can massage your shoulders and neck for yourself. Release mounting tension in these areas before your shoulders become permanently hunched up around your ears.

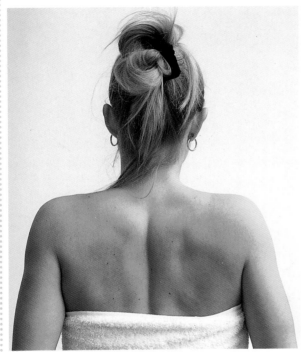

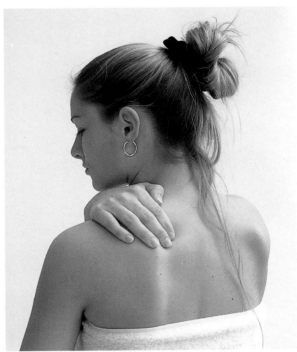

1 Shrug your shoulders and at the same time push them back as far as possible, hold for a count of 5 and then relax completely. Repeat five times.

2 Starting at the top of your arm, knead firmly, moving slowly towards your neck. Repeat the movements in the opposite direction back to the edge of your shoulder. Repeat three times on either side.

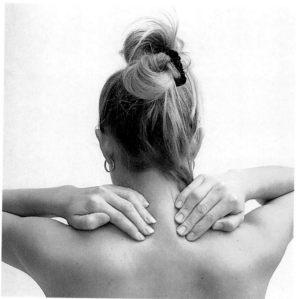

3 Press the back of your neck with the fingers of both hands and move your fingertips in an outward circular motion. Start at your shoulders and work up to the base of the skull. Repeat five times.

4 Gently hold your head and position your thumbs so that they are at the base of the skull. Rotate your thumbs, using moderate pressure. Do ten rotations, rest your arms and then repeat twice more.

Left: Scented candles can add a meditative touch to a room.

Burning aromatherapy oils or scented candles while being massaged provides a pleasantly scented atmosphere to the room and is a wonderful way to relax. The best essential oils to induce relaxation are lavender, chamomile and marjoram. Try not to use the same oil for more than two weeks at a time or you will find it becomes less effective.

MASSAGE WITH A PARTNER

One of the most reliable ways to relax and unwind (you may find your partner drifts off to sleep), a back massage releases much of the tension that accumulates through the day. Make sure there are no draughts in the room and that your partner is warm and comfortable. The oils you are using should be warm and close at hand before you begin so that you do not have to interrupt the session once you have begun. Remember to warm your hands first.

1 Use a smooth, stroking movement downwards with the thumbs on either side of the spine (not pressing on the bones, just outside them) and then take the hands to the side and glide back up to the shoulders. Repeat several times.

When preparing for a massage, make sure you have everything to hand so that you are not interrupted.

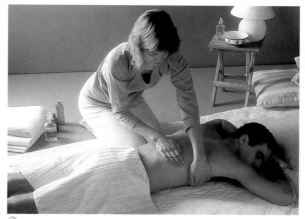

2 From a kneeling position at your partner's side, use the whole of your hands in a smooth stroking movement to pull up steadily, one hand at a time, working all the way up and down one side of the back a few times. Repeat from the other side.

3 Squeeze the muscles from one hand to the other, to knead the muscles of the back and shoulder and release deep-seated tension. Make sure you knead generously rather than using a pinching movement. Repeat on the other side.

4 Stretch the back, using your forearms to glide in opposite directions. Try to keep a constant, steady pressure. Lift the arms off when they reach the neck and buttocks, return to the centre of the back and repeat a few times.

Essential oils should be stored in dark glass dropper bottles in a cool, dark place. Blend only a small quantity of oils at a time to prevent deterioration.

RELAXING YOUR MIND

The tensions of modern working practices often mean that you are so caught up in meeting all the demands placed upon you that you maintain a high level of mental and physical activity throughout your waking hours.

MEDITATION AND A BUSY WORK LIFE

A busy work schedule means that you are prone to cutting off your emotional responses and your enjoyment of the simple things in life, and pushing your physical and mental health to the limit. To counteract this pressure, you need periods of mental and physical relaxation at different stages in the day. By taking such time out, you will actually gain rather than lose in productivity.

In taking a break every 90 minutes or so, you should aim to change your mind/body state completely. Ideally, stop all work activity and change your physical position (standing rather than sitting, looking into the distance rather than close up, for example) and mental

focus. A 20-minute meditation is ideal, as it is the best form of total relaxation. On returning to work, you will see things afresh and deal with them more efficiently. The feeling of well-being will continue well into the next 90-minute period.

THE BENEFITS OF MEDITATION

Meditation is a pleasant way to gain deep relaxation with time and space to yourself. Just meditating on a regular basis can be beneficial, but using some simple words and images while you meditate can promote an improvement in your general well-being or in a specific area of your life. The mind ceases to be a burden and distraction and instead becomes a tool for paying full attention to the present moment. In this way, meditation practice becomes relevant to real life. The physical benefits include relaxation, improvement of sleeping patterns, lowering of high blood pressure and speedier recovery from fatigue.

Above: Meditate in the bath if you have no time elsewhere.
Right: Adopt any position in which you feel at ease.

BREATHING TO CALM THE MIND

Your breath provides an ever-present and easily accessible focus for concentration: we are always breathing! Concentrating your attention on regular, quiet breathing is both physically calming and helps to clear your mind of any intrusive thoughts as an aid to meditation. Meditation can be as simple as just breathing while sitting.

IMPROVING YOUR RESPIRATORY AWARENESS

Your emotional state is reflected by your breathing patterns. When you are nervous or under strain, you may tend either to hyperventilate (over-breathe) or to inhale short, shallow breaths – a habit that you can only break when your attention is drawn to it. Take stock and examine the way you are breathing: is your breathing pattern regular and steady? If not, take a couple of deep breaths and start again, this time making a conscious effort to breathe steadily. Think about your breathing regularly to check it is still steady.

ALTERNATE NOSTRIL BREATHING

Practise these exercises to become aware of each breath and to help your breathing become more rhythmical and steady. Stop if you feel dizzy.

1 Place the first two fingers of one hand on your forehead, with thumb and third finger reaching down on either side of your nose.

2 Relax your thumb and inhale through that nostril; pinch it closed again, then release the finger to exhale through the other nostril.

3 Breathe in on the same side, then close that nostril and breathe out on the other side. Continue to breathe slowly and steadily through alternate nostrils.

WAYS OF GAINING THE MEDITATIVE STATE

Make a time and space you can call your own and use breathing and relaxation exercises
to ease yourself into the meditative state.

SOUNDS

An effortless sound, repeated with the natural rhythm of breathing, can have the same soothing, mentally liberating effect as the constant natural sound of running water, rustling leaves or a beating heart. The single sound, or "mantra", is used to blot out the chatter of intrusive thoughts, allowing the mind to find repose. The simple, gentle sound "om" or "aum" is sometimes known as the first mantra.

However, the sound need not be a special word; something simple and meaningful will be just as effective. The sound of the word "calm" spoken or thought with each outward breath can work very, very well, especially while imagining tension leaving your body and a calmness developing. Any word that appeals to you will do, repeated with the flow of breath. This clears the mind, slows the breathing and allows relaxation, both mental and physical, to develop.

Above: Repeating a simple sound or word,
such as "aum" or "calm", helps
clear the mind.

TOUCH

You can use your sense of touch in a lulling, soothing way to induce a state of meditation when you are under stress. You can witness young children doing this when they adopt a satisfyingly smooth ribbon or piece of fabric to hold and rub when they are feeling tense.

All over the Middle East, strings of worry beads are rhythmically passed through the fingers at difficult moments to focus the mind and calm anxiety. Their uniform size, gentle round shapes, smooth surfaces and rhythmic, orderly clicking as they are passed from hand to hand all assist the meditative state.

Use one or two smooth, round stones in the same way, passing them from hand to hand, and focusing your concentration on their temperature, shape and surfaces, or find an object with a tactile quality that particularly appeals to you (such as a piece of sculpture) to gently stroke.

153

MEDITATIONS: GUIDED PROGRAMMES

You may find it helpful to record the following meditation exercises on tape,
so that you can concentrate on gaining the images, or focusing attention, without worrying
about forgetting a passage or having to refer to the page.

THE HAVEN: YOUR OWN SPECIAL PLACE

Once you have managed to achieve complete physical relaxation and calm, allow your mind to enter a place, whether real or imaginary, that is special to you.

Now you can allow your mind to drift…drift to a pleasant, peaceful place. A place where you always feel able to relax…completely. A safe…secure…place where no one…and nothing…can ever bother you.

It may be a place you have visited on holiday, a beach or a place in the countryside. Or it may be a room…a room you have had…a room you do have…or a room you would like to have…an imaginary place. But it is a place where you can always feel able to let go…completely…a haven.

In order to help you imagine this place…notice first the light: is it bright, natural or dim…is there any particular source of light…natural or artificial? Notice also the temperature…hot, warm or cool…and any particular source of heat. Be aware of the colours that surround you…shapes…and textures.

You can just be there…whether sitting, lying or reclining, enjoying the sounds…the smells…the atmosphere…with nobody wanting anything, nobody needing anything and no one expecting or demanding anything from you…you can truly relax.

Left: Sitting on a pretty garden seat can be very restful.

Above: Visit your own special place, real or imaginary, where you can be truly safe and relaxed.

A CLOCK TICKING

The hands of a clock record the passage of time – time never stands still, although our perception of time can change. Past – present – future, the clock registers the moments of life moving forward.

The clock ticks…the hands move…so slowly… always moving…seconds tick away. The one just passed is over…a new one takes its place…it too is replaced…as time moves on…each moment lasts only a second. The clock may stop…time…never stops, it moves on…the moment that is over is out of reach… the moment to come has not arrived, yet. This moment is mine…this moment I can use as I wish… I focus on this moment…I influence this moment… I can use this moment…and no other now.

MEDITATION TO REDUCE STRESS

Visualization can be a great help in coping with stress. The imagination can stimulate emotions that can register new attitudes in the mind to provide a powerful influence for improvements in your overall confidence.

Above: While concentrating on relaxing the body, stress and fatigue are dispelled.

THE PROTECTIVE BUBBLE

Imagine yourself in a situation that has in the past caused you to feel stressed or anxious. Picture the situation, and any other people that might have been involved. See yourself there…and notice a slight shimmer of light between yourself and those other people…a sort of bubble around you…a protective bubble that reflects any negative feelings back to them…leaving you able to get on with your tasks… your life, with an inner strength and calmness.

Concentrate on this protective bubble that surrounds and protects you at all times. It will only allow those feelings that are positive and helpful to you to pass through for you to enjoy and build upon. Others may catch stress from each other… negativity, too, can be infectious…but you are protected…you continue to keep things in perspective…and to deal with things calmly and methodically. You are able to see the way forward clearly…solve problems…find ways around difficulties …by using your own inner resources and strengths, born of experience.

Now see yourself talking to someone who has been causing pressure to build. Find yourself knowing just how to let them know that what they are doing, or saying, is unhelpful in resolving the problem or difficulty. Find yourself able to let them know in such a way that they can accept your comments without offence…and find your own calmness and control…a strength that supports you.

You can let someone know if too much is being expected, and explain why. See yourself in that situation…calmly explaining the areas of difficulty…being able to supply examples and information until they understand the position. At all times you are surrounded by that protective bubble of light that keeps you calm and quietly confident, thinking everything through clearly and explaining it simply to others.

Next, imagine pushing out through that same protective bubble emotions that are unhelpful…past resentments…and hurts…embarrassments, too. You push them out through the bubble…where they can no longer limit or harm you. You are now better able to control the way you feel and react. The bubble stays with you, protecting you and and enabling you to remain in control…keeping things in perspective…having the strength to change those things you can change…accept those things you cannot…and move on with more confidence and happiness.

Above: Imagine yourself inside a bubble of calmness and strength protecting you from stress.

Natural Remedies for Stress

One of the main principles of natural medicine is the holistic approach, taking into account the physical, mental, emotional and indeed spiritual well-being of a person when assessing health problems: this is most obviously appropriate when dealing with nervous disorders such as anxiety and stress. Physical symptoms, such as headaches and insomnia, and emotional ones, such as depression and mental strain, can all weave together to create disease, or rather, dis-ease - a lack of harmony.

In order to help reduce the impact of stress on the whole system, you need to find ways both to avoid getting over-stressed in the first place and to let go of the changes that occur internally under stress. Gentle, natural remedies can help in each case, helping to keep you calm under pressure and releasing inner tensions. Herbal remedies are almost certainly the most popular method of self-help for minor complaints: infusions are a pleasant and safe way to take them and will alleviate many of the common symptoms of stress; you will find numerous simple recipes to help you in this book. Homeopathic remedies may also be effective as self-help, or you may benefit from a consultation with a qualified homeopath if a basic imbalance in your constitution needs addressing.

The art of aromatherapy harnesses the pure essences of aromatic plants, flowers and resins to work on the most powerful of the senses to restore the harmony of body and mind. It is well established that scent can evoke memories, change people's moods and make them feel good. Aromatherapy oils can be incorporated into massage, used in baths or evaporated into the air in a burner to improve physical and emotional well-being. To prevent undue stress, try simply inhaling one of your favourite essential oils at regular intervals to keep you feeling more relaxed and calm.

USING ESSENTIAL OILS

Aromatic essential oils may be used in many ways to maintain and restore health, and to improve the quality of life with their scents. Essential oils are concentrated substances and need to be diluted for safety and optimum effect. Treat them with care and respect – and allow them to treat you!

Above: Rose is one of the most complex of all the essential oils, ideal as a general tonic and fortifier.

MIXING OILS FOR MASSAGE

Massage is a wonderful way to use essential oils, diluted in a good base oil. Suitable base oils include sweet almond oil (probably the most versatile and useful), grapeseed, safflower, soya (a bit thicker and stickier), coconut and even sunflower. For very dry skins, a small amount of jojoba, avocado or wheat germ oils (except in cases of wheat allergy) may be added. Blend essential oils at a dilution of 1 per cent, or one drop per 5 ml/1 tsp base oil; this may sometimes be increased to 2 per cent, but take care that no skin reactions occur with any oil.

CAUTION
• Never take essential oils internally, unless professionally prescribed.
• Always use essential oils diluted – normally 1 per cent for massage; just 5 drops in a bath or for a steam inhalation.
• Do not use the same oils for too long: follow the "1–2 rule"; use one or two oils together, for not more than one or two weeks at any one time.
• Do not use oils in pregnancy, without getting professional advice; some oils, such as basil, clary sage, juniper, marjoram and sage, are contra-indicated at this time.

Above: Get your partner to massage you with a relaxing blend of essential oils as the perfect antidote to an overdose of life's stresses.

SCENTED ROOMS

You can create an aromatic environment, at home or in the workplace, by using essential oils in a vaporizer to disperse their beneficial aromas into the air. They can help to prevent ill-health and to balance the emotions, as well as freshening the atmosphere.

Rose, geranium, orange and lavender are pleasing and uplifting scents for a living room, used individually or blended together; bergamot is an excellent anti-depressant. At work, lemon helps efficiency while rosemary is a great aid to concentration.

BATHS

Soak in a warm bath, enveloped in delicious scent, and feel all the day's tensions melt away. Pour in 5 drops of your chosen blend just before you get into the water. The oils will be partly absorbed by your skin while you breathe in the scent, producing an immediate psychological and physiological effect.
• For a refreshing, uplifting morning bath, blend 3 drops bergamot and 2 drops geranium.
• To relax and unwind after a long day, blend 3 drops lavender and 2 drops ylang ylang.
• For tired, tense muscles, blend 3 drops marjoram and 2 drops chamomile.

Above: Lavender-scented candles can be relaxing.

RELAXING AND UPLIFTING ESSENTIAL OILS

Essential oils may be extracted from exotic plants such as sandalwood or ylang ylang, or from more common plants like lavender and chamomile, but each one has its own characteristics and properties. For the best results, use only the finest oils, bought from a reputable source.

BERGAMOT (*Citrus bergamia*)
The peel of the ripe fruit yields an oil that is mild and gentle. It is the most effective antidepressant of all, best used at the start of the day. Do not use on the skin before going into bright sunlight, as it increases photosensitivity.

CHAMOMILE (*Chamomilla recutita*)
Chamomile is relaxing and antispasmodic, helping to relieve tension headaches, nervous digestive problems and insomnia.

CLARY SAGE (*Salvia sclarea*)
This oil gives a definite euphoric uplift to the brain; do not use too much, however, as you can be left feeling very spacey! Like ylang ylang and jasmine, its antidepressant and relaxing qualities have contributed to its reputation as an aphrodisiac.

FRANKINCENSE (*Boswellia thurifera*)
The essence is spicy, with undertones of camphor, but becomes lemony when mixed with myrrh. It also blends well with sandalwood. Frankincense is warming and relaxing and is an excellent aid to meditation, as it deepens and slows the breath.

GERANIUM (*Pelargonium graveolens*)
The rose-scented geranium has very useful properties, not least being its ability to bring a blend together to make a more harmonious scent. Geranium has a refreshing, antidepressant quality, good for nervous tension and exhaustion.

JASMINE (*Jasminum officinale*)
An ancient favourite of the Arabs, Indians and Chinese, jasmine has a wonderful aroma with a relaxing, euphoric effect. It can greatly lift the mood when there is debility, depression and listlessness.

LAVENDER (*Lavandula angustifolia/officinalis*)
One of the safest and most versatile of all essential oils, lavender has been used for centuries as a refreshing fragrance and as a remedy for stress-related ailments. It is especially helpful for tension headaches or for nervous digestive systems. Use in a massage blend or in the bath for a deeply relaxing and calming experience.

LEMON (*Citrus limon*)
Possibly the most cleansing and antiseptic of the citrus oils, useful for boosting the immune system and in skin care. It can also refresh and clarify thoughts.

MARJORAM (*Origanum majorana*)
Marjoram has a calming, warming effect, and is good for both cold, tight muscles and for cold, tense people who may suffer from headaches, migraines and insomnia. Use in massage blends for tired, aching muscles, or in the bath, especially in the evening to encourage a good night's sleep.

NEROLI (*Citrus aurantium*)
Neroli is one of the finest of the floral essences. Its effect is uplifting and calming, bringing a feeling of peace. It is useful during times of anxiety, panic, hysteria or shock and fear. It can help in the development of self-esteem and is particularly effective for nervous diarrhoea and other stress-related conditions.

ORANGE (*Citrus aurantium*)
Refreshing but sedative, orange is a tonic for anxiety and depression, having a similar effect to neroli, which is distilled from the blossom of the same plant. Orange also stimulates the digestive system and is effective for constipation. Because the oil oxidizes very quickly, it cannot be kept for very long.

ROSE (*Rosa* x *damascena trigintipetala*)
The scent evokes a general sense of pleasure and happiness. The actions of the oil are sedating, calming and anti-inflammatory. Not surprisingly, rose oil has a wide reputation as an aphrodisiac, and where anxiety is a factor it can be very beneficial. Add to a base massage oil to soothe muscular and nervous tension.

ROSEMARY (*Rosmarinus officinalis*)
With a very penetrating, stimulating aroma, rosemary has been used for centuries to help relieve nervous exhaustion, tension headaches and migraines. It improves circulation to the brain and is an excellent oil for mental fatigue and debility. Avoid in cases of high blood pressure. Pregnant women should also avoid rosemary oil as it stimulates the uterus and can cause miscarriage.

SANDALWOOD (*Santalum album*)
Probably the oldest perfume in history, sandalwood is known to have been used for over 4,000 years. It has a relaxing, antidepressant effect on the nervous system, and where depression causes sexual problems sandalwood can be a genuine aphrodisiac.

YLANG YLANG (*Cananga odorata*)
This intensely sweet essential oil has a sedative yet antidepressant action. It is good for many symptoms of excessive tension, such as insomnia, panic attacks, anxiety and depression. It also has a reputation as an aphrodisiac, through its ability to reduce stress levels.

RELIEVING THE SYMPTOMS OF STRESS

The involuntary or autonomic nervous system has two divisions. The parasympathetic system is responsible for the body's "house-keeping", ensuring good digestion, assimilation of nutrients, detoxification and elimination of waste products. The sympathetic part prepares you for action and initiates the "fight or flight" response – making the heart and lungs more active and suppressing processes such as digestion and elimination. These mechanisms were originally developed to cope with potentially life-threatening situations, but nowadays are all too often brought into play by other factors, from meeting deadlines to receiving a stack of bills to pay.

If you are subject to too much stimulation, sympathetic activities become dominant or habitual and may reach a state of exhaustion, reducing your ability to react to new stresses

Above: A hot bath, calming herbal tea and a book to read can all work wonders on your stress levels.

that may arise. This stressed state can cause forgetfulness, panic, insomnia, exhaustion or vulnerability to infection. The converse problem is reduced parasympathetic activity, which can cause all sorts of digestive and nutritional debilities as well as poor elimination, resulting in problems with the skin, muscles or joints.

So stress can give rise to a host of physical as well as emotional problems, which will in turn weaken your body's performance and therefore your ability to cope with everyday pressure. Stressful events are likely to disrupt your appetite and your ability to rest, but both are vital to enable you to cope well. Natural therapies can offer help with many stress-related problems, to help you escape this vicious cycle and come through a difficult time.

Right: Steam inhalations can be deeply relaxing and soothing.

TENSION RELIEVERS

When you are under stress your centre of gravity tends to shift from the abdominal area up to the chest, causing tension in the neck and shoulders and often resulting in a feeling of a heaviness on your shoulders. Imagine how wonderful it would be to have someone touch these areas and relieve some of the pain and discomfort. To complete your Shiatsu session, pay some attention to these specific areas of your partner, or give your friend at work a neck and shoulder treatment there and then, in a chair.

TUNING IN

▲ Sit down in the Seiza position at your partner's head. Place your hands on the shoulders and tune in. Be aware of the breathing and state of relaxation before you start. Ask your partner to breathe in and on the exhalation apply a bit of pressure to the shoulders by leaning into your arms. Repeat a few times. This opens up the chest and encourages relaxation.

KNEADING THE SHOULDERS

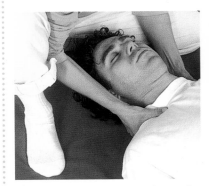

▲ With your fingers underneath and thumbs on top, gently and firmly massage the shoulders using a kneading action. Feel the tension in the muscles relaxing and the tissue gradually softening up.

NECK STRETCH

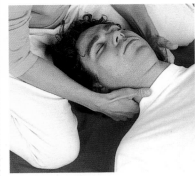

▲ Move your hands to the neck. With your thumbs on the side and fingers underneath, stretch out the neck by gently pulling away. Repeat a few times until you feel the neck muscles relax.

SQUEEZING THE NECK

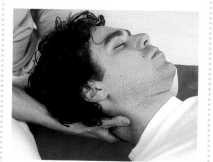

▲ Lift your partner's head off the floor and firmly squeeze the muscles of the neck.

RELEASING MUSCLE TENDONS

▲ Turn the head to one side and support it with one hand. Use the finger pads of your other hand to "rub" across the muscle fibres. Treat the other side of the head in the same way.

STIMULATING POINTS ALONG THE BASE OF THE SKULL

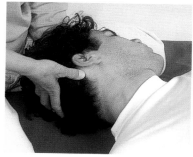

▲ With your partner's head turned to the side, press the points along the base of the skull. Start at the ear and work towards the spine. Turn the head and treat the other side in the same way.

STIMULATING THE SCALP

▲ Rub the scalp using your fingertips and then run your fingers through the hair.

NECK STRETCH

▲ Turn your partner's head to one side and support it by placing one hand at the base of the skull.

Cross your other arm over and place it on your partner's shoulder. Ask your partner to breathe in; on the out-breath, stretch this side of the neck by gently and gradually pushing the shoulder down towards the feet, keeping the other hand still. Repeat a couple of times, making sure your partner feels the stretch. Repeat on the other side of the neck.
Caution *Listen to your partner during this stretch, and take care not to cause injury.*

INSTANT REVITALIZERS

Chronic tension all too often leads to a feeling of exhaustion, when you just run out of steam. When you need to be bright and alert before an important meeting, a long drive or a party, try these simple exercises to give you that instant tonic to set you on your feet again.

SELF-MASSAGE: ARMS, SHOULDERS AND NECK

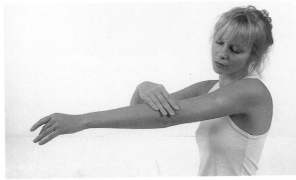

1 Do a kneading action on the arms, working rapidly from the wrist to the shoulder and back again with a firm squeezing movement.

2 Rub swiftly up the outside of each arm to stimulate the circulation. Work in an upwards direction each time to encourage blood flow back to the heart.

3 With the fingers and thumb of one hand, firmly squeeze the neck muscles, using a circular motion.

Above: Mandarin oil is very invigorating.

SELF-MASSAGE: LEGS AND BUTTOCKS

1 Sitting down, with one leg raised slightly, stroke the leg with both hands from ankle to thigh. Begin the stroke as close to the ankle as you can reach. Repeat several times, moving around the leg slightly each time to stroke a different part.

2 Massage the knee, slowly stroking around the outside of the kneecap to begin with, then using circular pressure with the fingertips to work around the kneecap more firmly.

3 Knead the calf muscle with both hands, using a firm *pétrissage* (squeezing action) to loosen any tension in the muscle.

4 Continue the kneading on the thigh, working over the top and outside areas with alternate hands. While the leg is still raised, do some soothing *effleurage* (firm strokes) up the back of the leg from ankle to hip. Repeat steps 1-4 on the other leg.

5 Kneel up and pummel your hips and buttocks, using a clenched fist and keeping your wrists flexible.

INVIGORATING OILS

Many oils have a tonic effect, restoring vitality without over-stimulating. As a group, the citrus oils are good for this purpose, ranging from the more soothing mandarin to the very refreshing lemon oil.

Have a warm but not too hot bath, with 4 drops mandarin and 2 drops orange or 4 drops neroli and 2 drops lemon. Alternatively, just add a couple of drops of any of these oils to a bowl of steaming water and gently inhale for 10 minutes, to lift your spirits.

MUSCLE FATIGUE RELIEVERS

When your legs and arms become very tired, either through general tension or muscle fatigue, the contraction of the muscles can lead to poor circulation to the extremities. This can become a vicious cycle, as the restricted blood flow fails to nourish the muscles adequately, leading them to stay in a more contracted state. One or two simple stretches can help to restore blood supply to the area, as well as relieving tight, cramped muscles.

CALF STRETCH
Sit on the floor with one leg out in front of you. Lean forwards and grasp the foot with your hand. Pull the foot gently towards you, feeling the tightness in the calf. If you are unable to hold the foot in this position, try doing this stretch with the leg slightly bent. Repeat with the other leg.

HAMSTRING STRETCH
Lie down flat, with one leg raised and the other knee bent. Stretch the muscle by pulling gently towards the chest. Relax, then repeat with the other leg.

CALF AND FOOT EXERCISE
Sit on the floor with both legs straight out in front of you, then alternately flex and extend each foot.

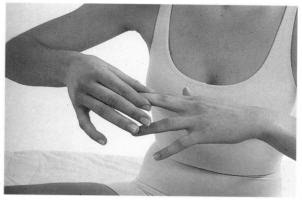

FINGER PULLS
Squeeze each finger joint between your finger and thumb. Then hold the base of each finger and pull the finger gently, sliding your grip up to the top of the finger in a continuous movement.

THERAPEUTIC OILS
Mix two or three essential oils in a base of sweet almond oil or jojoba oil. The quantities given are for a 50ml/¼ cup bottle of base oil. Add 20 drops of the mixed oil to the bath, or as required for massage.
ANTI-STRESS MIX
10 drops each of marjoram, lavender and sandalwood.
UPLIFTING MIX
5 drops rosemary, 5 drops camphor, 20 drops peppermint.

Right: Home-made oils are effective and easy to make.

CAUTION
If someone has sensitive skin or suffers from allergies, then try massaging with just 1 drop of essential oil per 20 ml/4 tsp of base oil at first to test for any reaction. Seek medical advice before massaging a pregnant woman.

BACKACHE RELIEVERS

The most common cause of lost time at work is backache. In the great majority of cases, back trouble is the result of chronic tensions which build up in the back. The stretches shown here, based on Yoga postures, are intended to aid flexibility of the spine, and should be performed gently and slowly, all the time breathing deeply.

LOWER BACK STRETCH

1 Lie on your front, with your arms bent so that your hands are directly under your shoulders, palms down.

2 Slowly lift your head and push down on your arms to help raise your trunk. Exhale as you raise your body.

3 If you can, tilt your head backwards and stretch up and back as far as possible. Hold briefly, then relax and lower your body back down. Repeat steps 1–3.

LOWER BACK TWIST

1 Sit on the floor with your legs straight out in front of you.

2 Bend one leg and place the foot on the floor across the other knee.

3 With your opposite arm, reach around the bent leg to catch hold of the straight leg, then twist your body. Repeat on the other side.

SIDE STRETCH

1 Stand with your feet shoulder-width apart and your arms stretched out to the sides.

2 Bend down to one side without twisting your body, letting the opposite arm rise in the air.

3 Stretch the raised arm, look up and hold. Slowly straighten and repeat on the other side.

CHEST HUG

1 To complete this sequence of exercises, relieve any strain in the back by lying on your back with legs bent up and hands clasped around the knees.

2 Lift your head and hug your legs into your chest, hold, then relax. Take care not to strain your neck when lifting your head.

CAUTION
If you have suffered a back injury or have back pain, seek medical advice before doing these stretches. Always stop any exercise immediately if you feel acute discomfort.

RELIEVING ANXIETY

Anxiety can produce many symptoms, including palpitations, sweating, irritability and sleeplessness. If it continues, it will deplete vital energy, leading to a general state of nervousness and tension. Tense muscles in the face can be released with a gentle face massage, especially using soothing strokes on the temples and forehead.

FACIAL MASSAGE

1 Starting in the centre of the forehead, make small circles with your fingertips, working outwards to the temples. Repeat three times.

2 Use your fingers to gently apply pressure to the area where the eye socket meets your nose. Repeat three times.

3 Move your fingers outwards along the brow bone from the top of your nose. Repeat five times.

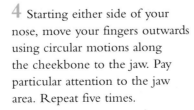

4 Starting either side of your nose, move your fingers outwards using circular motions along the cheekbone to the jaw. Pay particular attention to the jaw area. Repeat five times.

For a calming face massage, make up a blend of 4 drops lavender and 2 drops ylang ylang in a light oil such as sweet almond, grapeseed or coconut. Always patch-test a new oil before using on your face.

DEALING WITH DEPRESSION

Just as with anxiety, depression can be due to several reasons, and the symptoms may be quite varied. Conditions like constipation, headaches, insomnia, loss of physical and mental energy and loss of appetite can all relate to depression. In deep or continuing instances of depression professional help is essential. This is especially so when there is no obvious reason for the feelings, a condition generally labelled endogenous depression.

UPLIFTING BATH OIL

For a strong but relatively short-lived effect, try 4 drops bergamot and 2 drops neroli essential oils in the bath, ideally in the morning. For a gentler effect, you could use either oil – one drop at a time – in an oil burner, to pervade the atmosphere all day long.

DIET AND EXERCISE

Overhaul the diet, reducing coffee, tea, sugar and alcohol. Eat plenty of wholefoods, especially salads, fruit and vegetables. Increase vegetable protein if it has been low. Taking exercise is a good step as it increases oxygen uptake and improves circulation.

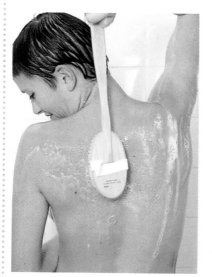

Above: Have an invigorating shower to help you face the day.

Above: Vegetables are an excellent source of vitamins and minerals. A well-nourished person copes better with life's ups and downs.

IMPROVING SELF-WORTH

Affirmations are a deceptively simple but effective device that anyone can use. Try to use them while in the meditative state, having previously planned and memorized the affirmations you wish to make. We all have attributes and qualities in which we can take pride and pleasure. Emphasize these positive aspects to allay the doubts that only serve to limit your potential. Affirmations can change the way you think about yourself and the way you act and react.

AFFIRMATIONS

This technique requires you to say to yourself, out loud, a positive statement about yourself as you wish to be. To make affirmations effective, they should:
• be made in the present tense;
• be positively phrased;
• have an emotional reward.
Yours is the most influential voice in your life, because you believe it! Be aware of any negative statements you regularly make about yourself – "I am shy," "I lack confidence," "I get nervous when…" and so on – they are self-limiting beliefs that you are reinforcing each time they slip into your conversation. You can use affirmations while meditating to change those beliefs.

• I like my (physical attribute).
• I am proud of my (attitude or achievement).
• I love meeting people – they are fascinating.
• My contribution is valuable to (name person).
• I am lovable and can give love.
• Others appreciate my (opinions, assistance, a personal quality).
• I enjoy being a unique combination of mind and body.

Imagine yourself speaking to colleagues, your boss, employees or friends…See yourself behaving and looking confident, standing and looking like a confident person…Notice how you stand…your facial expression…hear the way that you speak… slowly, calmly, quietly and clearly.

Above: Improving your self-worth will enable you to fully enjoy the company of loved ones.

Right: Value yourself and your positive features.

GETTING A GOOD NIGHT'S SLEEP

Sleeplessness is a common response to stress, as your mind and body refuse to let go enough to give you the rest you need. The resulting disturbed and restless night leaves you more prone to stress and anxiety, and a vicious cycle can be created. Learning to relax has to be built into a daily pattern based on a healthy diet, regular exercise and a calming routine to wind down before bedtime.

SLEEP ENHANCERS

In order to get the proper rhythm of energy through the day, it is useful to get plenty of exercise and get fresh air in the daytime. It may help to get up fairly early in the morning as well to restore this balance. Do not sleep in a stuffy room, or drink coffee, tea or cola at night, a hot milky drink would be a pleasant and soothing alternative.

AROMATHERAPY OILS FOR A RESTFUL SLEEP

Essential oils are a very pleasant and effective means of unwinding and aiding restful sleep – try using them in the bath – or else putting 2-3 drops on to a paper tissue under the pillow at night. Choose from the following, either using a single oil or a blend; do not use the same single oil for more than 2 weeks or you will find it becomes less effective.

Chamomile: calming and relaxing, good where indigestion contributes to broken sleep.

Lavender: very soothing, and also analgesic, very suitable if any aches or pains contribute to insomnia.

Marjoram: relaxing and warming, in large amounts it is quite sedating but can leave you feeling a bit thick-headed in the morning, if overdone.

Left: A calming routine to wind-down before bedtime.

A GENTLE WAVE

These massage strokes wash over the limbs in outward flowing motions, creating a gentle stream of movement. The soft, downward strokes have a hypnotic and sedative effect, and brief pauses in the motion create a lovely, wave-like feeling. Repeat each movement up to five times on each part of the body.

1 Place one hand over the chest, and the other over the back of the shoulder. As you breathe in, pull your hands steadily outwards and down to the edge of the shoulder. Pause briefly as you exhale, lightly cradling the top of the arm.

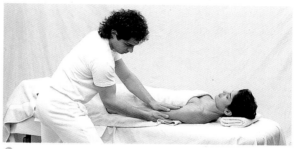

2 Continue the pulling motion down the length of the arm. As you breathe in, pull both hands down to just below the elbow joint. Relax as you breathe out, then continue the slide down the forearm and below the wrist.

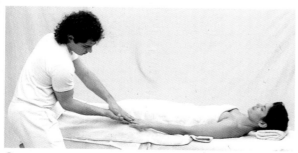

3 Draw your hands over both sides of your partner's hand and fingers, taking your stroke out beyond the body as the hand settles back on to the mattress. Repeat steps 1–3 on the other side of the body.

4 Pull your hands down over the hips and down the leg to just below the knee. Continue this wave-like motion down the lower leg to the ankle, then pull gently and steadily out over the toes. Repeat this sequence of strokes on the other side of the body.

LIBIDO ENHANCER: SENSUAL MASSAGE

Stress at work, or in daily life, can affect normal sexual functioning. This massage, as well as releasing stresses and tensions from the muscles, is a wonderful way to enhance a relationship, and nurture the caring, sharing touch, which is invaluable in coping with stressful situations. It is important to take a little extra time to create the right environment, to make the whole experience a real treat – time for you both in a hurried world. Make the room extra warm, get your partner to be minimally clothed or to undress fully, and just be covered with warm towels, perhaps play some of your favourite, soothing music and have soft lighting or better still, work in candle light. Stroking movements should be the mainstay of a sensual massage. Use a little more oil than usual to help them flow more easily. At the end, your partner may of course just fall asleep.

1 Effleurage is a classic stroking movement. Place your hands on either side of the spine, but not on it, and glide down the back. Move out to the sides and up the back again. Repeat several times.

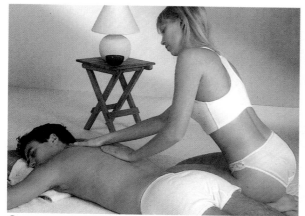

2 With a gentle motion, stroke down the centre of the back with one hand following the other smoothly, as if you were stroking a cat.

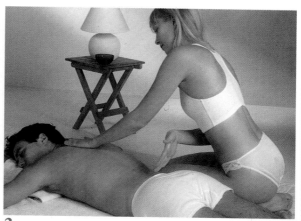

3 As one hand lifts off at the pelvis, start again with the other hand at the neck.

4 Place both your hands on the upper back and stroke outwards in a fan shape.

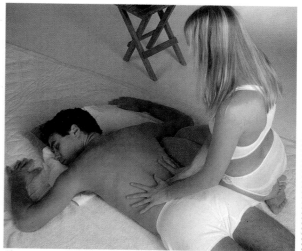

5 Work down the back, including the buttocks, using the fanning action.

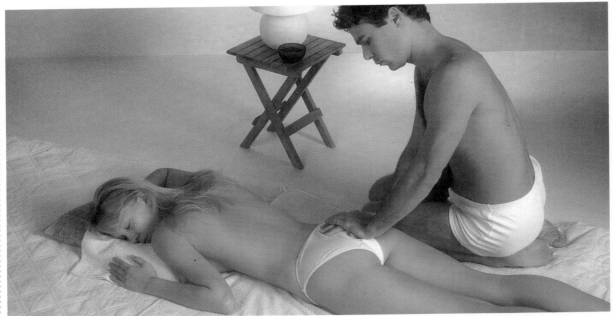

6 Use a firm, steady circling action on the buttocks. These are large, powerful muscles that may be able to take a little more pressure if your partner desires, but avoid giving any discomfort.

7 Stroke up the back of the legs, with one hand after the other in a smooth, flowing motion.

8 As one hand reaches the buttocks, start on the calf with the other to keep a steady rhythm.

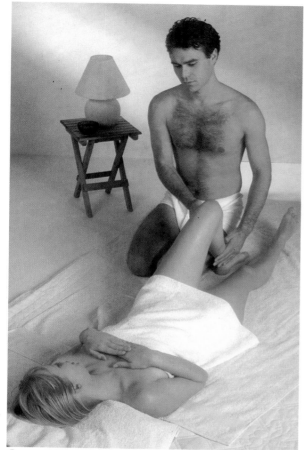

9 Turn your partner over and stroke up the front of the legs; having the leg bent helps the muscles relax.

10 Continue the movement, using both hands to stroke from the knees up the thighs.

11 Effleurage may also be used on the front of the body, kneeling from the head end. Be careful not to press in with your thumbs. All these movements should make for a truly sensual experience, and help to put your partner back in touch with his or her body – and maybe yours too.

REDUCING OFFICE TENSION

For people who spend their working day sitting at a desk, whether at home or in an office, it is very easy to get stiff and aching muscles. As we get tired, our posture suffers and we can find ourselves becoming round-shouldered. Try these simple stretches while sitting at your desk.

1 Link your hands together, palms away from your body, and push your arms straight out in front of you. Hold for a few seconds, relax and repeat.

2 Link your hands together behind your back, over the top of the chair, and lift your arms slightly. Push away from your body, hold, then repeat.

3 Stretch your arms straight out to the sides. Alternately flex and extend your hands, feeling the pull on the upper and lower sides of your forearms.

4 Bend forwards and clasp your ankles. Arch your back to stretch, relax and repeat.

5 Sitting upright, lift and straighten each leg alternately. Flex the foot to stretch the calf muscle. Repeat a few times.

7 Finally, link your fingers together and stretch your arms high above your head.

6 Slowly turn your head from side to side, feeling the extension in the neck muscles.

Many office chairs are not good for the posture, and long hours spent staring at a computer screen can give your neck, upper and lumber back muscles a very hard time. Regular breaks help: get up and walk around every now and then.

FOR CONFIDENCE IN FUTURE SITUATIONS

The meditative state, affirmations and visualization can be a valuable rehearsal and preparation for a future event. Athletes and other sports people have proved that it works. We can all use this process to achieve our own optimum performance in any situation.

• I am quietly confident in meetings
• I speak slowly, quietly and confidently so that others listen
• My contribution is wanted and valued by others
• I enjoy meetings, as they bring forth new ideas and renew my enthusiasm

Imagine a meeting that is about to happen, and see yourself there, filling in all the details that you know, and the people too; imagine yourself there looking confident and relaxed, concentrating on what is happening. Be aware of the acute interest you are giving to what is happening, complete, concentrated attention, and then imagine yourself speaking, to give information or to ask a question: hear yourself speaking quietly, slowly and calmly . . . Notice people listening to what you are saying; they wish you well and support you, as you are expressing your viewpoint or raising a question they may well have wanted to ask, too. Notice how you are sitting or standing, how you lean slightly forward when speaking . . . that expression of calm confidence on your face. When this is clear in your mind, just like a film playing in your mind's eye, play it back and forth. When you are feeling comfortable with it, get into that imaginary you, "climb aboard" and be there in your mind, seeing things from that perspective, hearing things from that point in the meeting. As you speak, get in touch with those calm feelings, and the attitudes that allow you to feel calm, in control, and quietly confident there . . . It is like a rehearsal; the more you rehearse the better the final performance will be. You will acquire the attitudes, stance and tone of voice, so that when you are in that situation all of these will be available to you, and it will be just as you imagined, as if you had done it all, successfully, before.

Imagine yourself at an important event where you are at ease.

The moment of initial introductions can be tense, but remember how you looked, stood and felt in your visualization.

The preparation was worth it, having given your best and feeling good about your performance.

Useful Addresses

HOMEOPATHY
UK
The Homeopathic Society
2 Powis Place
Great Ormond Street
London
WC1N 3HT

The Society of Homeopaths
2 Artizan Road
Northampton
NN1 4HU

OUTLETS FOR HOMEOPATHIC
REMEDIES

Most chemists and health food shops
will stock a limited supply of homeopathic remedies. The list below will
stock a complete range.

Buxton and Grant
176 Whiteladies Road
Bristol
BS8 2XU

Freeman's Pharmacy
7 Eaglesham Road
Clarkston
Glasgow
G76 7BU

Goulds the Chemist
14 Crowndale Road
London
NW1 1TT

Helios Pharmacy
97 Camden Road
Tunbridge Wells
Kent
TN1 2QR

US
Homeopathic Educational Services
2124 Kittredge Street
Berkeley
CA 94704

National Center for Homeopathy
801 N Fairfax No 306
Alexandria
VA 22314

AUSTRALIA
Australian Institute of Homeopathy
PO Box 122
Roseville
NSW 2069

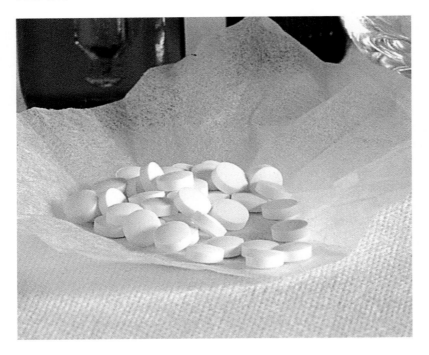

HERBALISM
UK
National Institute of Medical
Herbalists
56 Longbrook Street
Exeter
Devon
EX4 6AH

The Herb Society
134 Buckingham Palace Road
London
SW1W 9SA

The School of Phytotherapy/Herbal
Medicine
Buckstreep Manor
Bodle Street Green
Hailsham
East Sussex
BN27 4RJ

US
The Herb Research Foundation
1007 Pearl Street
Suite 200
Boulder
CO 80302

American Botanical Council
PO Box 144345
Austin
TX 78714

Blazing Star Herb School
PO Box 6
Shelburne Falls
MA 01370

OUTLETS FOR HERBS
Cameron Park Botanicals
Highway 64 East
Raleigh
NC 27610

Caprilands Herb Farm
Silver Street
North Coventry
CT 06238

Seeds Blum
Idaho City State
Boise
ID 83706

AUSTRALIA
National Herbalist Association
PO Box 61
Broadway
NSW 2066

INDEX

abdomen, loosening-up exercises,
    141, 144
abscesses, 44
Aconite, 58
affirmations, 176, 186
allergies, 46-7
Allium cepa, 58
anaemia, 50
Ant tart, 58
anxiety, 55, 118-19, 174
Apis, 59
Arg nit, 59
arms: loosening-up exercises, 141
    self-massage, 168
Arnica, 59
aromatherapy, 160-3
Arsenicum, 60

babies, homeopathy, 48-9
back, loosening-up exercises, 145
backache relievers, 172-3
baths, essential oils, 161, 171

Belladonna, 60
bergamot oil, 162
bites and stings, 34-5
boils, 44
borage, 93
breathing, calming the mind, 152
bruises, 32
Bryonia, 60
burns, 34
"butterflies", calming, 126
buttocks, self-massage, 169
buying herbs, 79

Calendula, 61
Cantharis, 66
chamomile, 88
chamomile oil, 162
Chamomilla, 66
chaste tree, 105
children, homeopathy, 48-9
clary sage oil, 162
clock ticking meditation, 155
Cocculus, 61
colds, 36-7, 120
colic, 49, 127
confidence, improving, 176, 186-7
constipation, 127
convalescence, 123
cooking with herbs, 84
coughs, 37, 120
cramp bark, 101

croup, 37, 49
culinary herbs, 84-5
cuts, 33
cystitis, 50

damiana, 100
decoctions, 81
dental treatment, 35
depression, 125, 175
digestives, herbal, 126-7
disease: causes, 19
    symptoms, 18, 21, 24-5
doctors, visiting, 35
Drosera, 62
drying herbs, 79

ear infections, 40
Echinacea, 30
emotional problems, 54-5
essential oils, 160-3
Eupatorium, 62
Euphrasia, 62
evening primrose, 106
exercise, 138
    loosening-up exercises, 140-5
eye problems, 41

facial massage, 174
fatigue relievers, 170-1
Ferrum phos, 63
fevers, 38-9, 48-9

first-aid, homeopathy, 26, 28-9, 32-5
flu, 36-7
flying, fear of, 35
fractures, 33
frankincense, 162
fright, 55

gastric upsets, 42
gathering herbs, 78
Gelsemium, 63
geranium oil, 162
ginseng, 91
grief, 54-5
growing herbs, 74-5, 78

Hahnemann, Samuel, 8
hangover remedies, 128
harvesting herbs, 78
haven, meditation, 154
hay fever, 47
head, tension reliever, 167
headaches, 129
Hepar sulph, 63
herbal remedies, 10-11, 110-131
homeopathy, 8-10, 15-71
hops, 94
hot flushes, 53
Hypericum, 64

Ignatia, 64
immune system, 20
indigestion, 43
insomnia, 55, 131, 178-9

Ipecac, 61

jasmine oil, 162

Kali bich, 64

Lachesis, 65
lady's mantle, 105
lavender, 102
lavender oil, 162
Ledum, 65
legs: fatigue relievers, 170-1
    loosening-up exercises, 142-3
    self-massage, 169
lemon balm, 89
lemon oil, 163
libido, revitalizing, 130, 180-3
licorice, 92
lime blossom, 107
loosening-up exercises, 140-5
Lycopodium, 65

Mag phos, 66
marjoram, 109
marjoram oil, 163
massage, 139, 148-9
    facial, 174
    instant revitalizers, 168-9
    oils, 160
    self-massage, 146-7
    sensual massage, 180-3
    for sleep problems, 179
mastitis, 50-1
Materia Medica, 24, 56-71

meditation, 150-7
    breathing, 152
    guided programmes, 154-7
    to reduce stress, 156-7
menopause, 53, 116
Mercurius, 67
mint, 108
motherwort, 104
mugwort, 98
muscles: fatigue relievers, 170-1
    loosening-up exercises, 140-5
    relaxing, 117
    tension reliever, 166-7

neck: loosening-up exercises, 140
    self-massage, 146-7, 168
    tension relievers, 166-7
neroli oil, 163
nervous exhaustion, 122
Nux vomica, 70

oats, wild, 100
office tension, 184-5

oils: aromatherapy, 160-3
    cold infused oils, 83
orange oil, 163
pasque flower, 109
passionflower, 96
period pains, 52, 115
Phosphorus, 67
Phytolacca, 67
poppy, Californian, 96
potentization, homeopathy, 23
pre-menstrual tension (PMT), 52,
    114
protective bubble, meditation,
    156-7
provings, homeopathy, 24
Pulsatilla, 68
puncture wounds, 33

reflexology, 139
relaxation, 117, 135, 138-57
remedies, homeopathic, 22-3
Rescue Remedy, 29, 71
revitalizers, instant, 168-9
Rhus tox, 68

rose oil, 163
rosemary, 103
rosemary oil, 163
Ruta, 68

sage, 97
St. John's Wort, 99
sandalwood oil, 163
Schussler, Wilhelm, 23
self-massage, 146-7
self-worth, improving, 176, 186-7
sensual massage, 180-3
Sepia, 69
shoulders: loosening-up exercises,
    140
    self-massage, 146-7, 168
    tension reliever, 166
Silica, 69
skullcap, 90
sleep problems, 55, 131, 178-9
sore throats, 38, 121
sounds, meditation, 153
Spongia, 69
sprains and strains, 33
stomach upsets, 42
storing herbs, 79
stress, 12-13
    coping strategies, 134-5
    herbal remedies, 112-13
    meditation, 156-7
    natural remedies, 158-63
    relieving symptoms, 164-85
Symphytum, 70
symptoms, 18, 21, 24-5

teas, herbal, 80
teething, 48
tension relievers, 166-7
throats, sore, 38, 121
tinctures, 82
tissue salts, 23
tonics, 123
toothache, 45
touch, meditation, 153
travel sickness, 35

Valerian, 70, 95
Verbascum, 71
vervain, 101
Viburnum opulus, 71
vital force, 20-1

wind, 43, 49, 127
winter blues, 124
women's health problems, 50-3
wood betony, 90
wounds, 33

ylang ylang oil, 163